segovia

andrés

segovia

an autobiography
of the years
1893-1920

translated by W. F. O'Brien

Macmillan Publishing Co., Inc.

NEW YORK

Edited by Tana de Gámez

Designed and illustrated by Vladimir Bobri

Macmillan Publishing Co., Inc.
866 Third Avenue, New York, N.Y. 10022
Collier Macmillan Canada, Ltd.

Library of Congress Cataloging in Publication Data

Segovia, Andrés, 1893–
     Andrés Segovia: an autobiography of the years 1893–1920.

     1. Segovia, Andrés, 1893–   2. Guitarists—Spain—Biography.
ML419.S4A39   787'.61'0924 [B]   76—42291
ISBN 0—02—609080—5

FIRST PRINTING 1976
Printed in the United States of America

to
my son

CARLOS
Andres

This lesson in dedication
and
perseverance

Andrés Segovia at the age of ten, in Granada. Drawing by Bobri.

Preface: Threshold

PERHAPS THE READER should dismiss these brief prefatory lines as unnecessary, since by glancing at any page of these memoirs he or she is bound to discover what I mean to say in them: namely, that this book was written by someone who did not have the fortune to receive a formal education: myself. I am a self-taught man. My scant knowledge is the product of deep and constant reading, done without method or discipline.

It is common today for people from all walks of life—football players, bullfighters, impresarios, even delinquents—to publish their biography signed by themselves but written by someone else. The procedure in such cases is to hire experienced craftsmen who work anonymously for a fee. I would not think of using a borrowed pen. I choose to use my own and speak in my own words. Thus, in lieu of scholarship and writing craft, the reader will find greater authenticity in this story.

This is the first book of an autobiography which may turn out to be more voluminous than luminous, as I often say. At times I fear I may have begun this difficult project rather late; the task may be beyond my strength, by now considerably diminished by the length and scope of my work, the rigors of travel, and the inevitable toll of passing years.

Still, I face the challenge cheerfully, happy in the thought that the account of my struggling career, with its examples of great patience and persevering will, may help young students overcome moments of discouragement and unjustified despair. I will trace the road I have traveled since my early youth, often having to surmount rather than skirt around great obstacles. However, the soothing light of my good star never failed to guide my steps and help me avoid deep falls and long retreats on the way to the goal I had set for myself.

Here, then, are the milestones of my struggle. I found the guitar almost at a standstill—despite the noble efforts of Sor, Tárrega, Llobet and others—and raised it to the loftiest levels of the music world. Although, at one time, the guitar lacked a legitimate or even a usable repertoire, today a surprising number of works have been and continue to be written for it by renowned composers. Conservatories and music schools of bygone days would not open their classrooms to students of this beautiful instrument. Today the guitar enjoys an honorable reception everywhere and is taught and encouraged in the highest music-learning centers of Paris, London, Zurich, Vienna, Milan, Rome, and major cities of North and South America. Yesterday the guitar would draw only small audiences mostly made up of aficionados more interested in the instrument than in music itself. Today the largest concert halls are too small to hold the vast audiences whose devotion to the guitar is not a passing vogue but a serious interest which grows and deepens year after year.

What pleases me above all is the fact that, with me or without me, the guitar continues forging ahead. My students, now teachers themselves, and their pupils—my scholastic grandchildren, so to speak—are imparting a new spirit to this poetic instrument. Ernest Renan, the French philologist, used to say —and I quote his idea, not his words—that he would give ten years of his life to see the titles of the books children would be taking to school at the turn of his century. I, too, would give much to be able to see a catalog of works written for the guitar by the turn of my century, to learn what technical developments and outstanding place the instrument will have achieved by then.

Detractors? The guitar still has them, notwithstanding the battles it has won in the most rarefied academic spheres. It does not matter; 'tis nobler for the mind to ignore such slings and arrows as have no power to wound.

I, for one, still stand fast at the ramparts, in and out of planes and tours and concert halls, adapting new and old works in my leisure time. And . . . I'll soon be eighty-three. "Hard work," as a sage once said, "is the strong man's means of self-destruction."

Something else. When the reader goes beyond the threshold to these memoirs, he or she will notice that there are no suggestive scenes in these pages. It would be highly distasteful to me to resort to such ends in order to enhance the commercial possibilities of this book. Besides, I have never thought of myself as a Don Juan. I have belonged to women more than they have belonged to me; in other words, it was I who was conquered by their charms. To expose bedroom intimacies would be as inelegant as it would be unfair to the ladies and damsels who may have delighted certain moments in our past—all the more should any of them have had a lasting influence in our life.

Enough. I pride myself only in having been a daring, tireless prober of the subtle beauty of the guitar, in conquering for it the love of millions in the world ahead.

——Andrés Segovia

segovia

I WAS BORN in Linares, Andalusia. Although not the most picturesque town, it is certainly one of the most prosperous in the rich province of Jaén, famous from ancient times for its silver and lead mines. The province is known today for the fertility of its soil, which produces excellent vegetables, exquisite fruit, and tasty olives.

A few weeks after my birth in 1893, my parents returned to their native city, Jaén. There the wind blows with such fury that it wrests harmonic sounds from the cathedral bells. Its violence must have affected my sensitive lungs and my parents, not wanting to be accused of sending my soul off to the gray world of limbo, took me at the brink of death to be baptized. "However," they were later fond of recalling, "he was strong enough to spit out the grains of coarse salt the priest put in his mouth. It was a good omen!"

I spent the first years of my life in Jaén, years which I can no longer remember, but I do recall the sad day when my parents left me in the care of my Uncle Eduardo and my Aunt Maria. They had no children of their own and lived in Villacarrillo, close to the parish house, on a street called *De las Barandas*. I was being taken from the living cradle of my mother's arms and I wept bitterly. Hoping to distract me, my uncle, bearded, completely bald and without a tooth in his head—sat down in front of me, and pretending to strum a guitar held to his chest, sang:

El tocar la guitarra	To play guitar
jum!	*jum!*
no tiene "cencia"	You need no "science"
jum!	*jum!*
sino "juerza" en el brazo	only a strong arm
jum!	*jum!*
Permanecencia	and perseverance
jum!	*jum!*

He repeated the ditty again and again until I calmed down and smiled back at him. Taking my small right arm, he made me beat the rhythm to the *"jum."* This gave me such an intense feeling of delight that even today, remembering it, my memory is suffused by a warm sensation.

This was the first musical seed to be cast in my soul and it was to develop, as time passed, into the strongest and most rewarding constant in my life.

My aunt and uncle soon noticed my early vocation. I was not yet six years old when they placed me under the tutorship of Don Francisco Rivera, a violinist of hard ear and stiffer fingers. He managed to convert my music lessons into my martyrdom. He pinched me and made me cry at the first sign of faulty intonation or rhythm so that I came both to fear the teacher and hate what he was trying to instill in me. Such were my feelings that his harshness could well have turned me away from a life in the arts. I could not remember my lessons and he declared me to be inept: "Neither memory, measure nor ear," was his verdict. My uncle, unconvinced, but with tact and good judgment, took me away from those sterile classes.

2

A strolling flamenco guitar player stopped in our town, worldly wise and opportunistic, who was told by neighbors that Don Eduardo, my uncle, would listen to him and might even put a few *pesetas* into his empty pockets. As a young man my uncle had been very fond of flamenco dance, music, and song. Indeed, he had spent a good part of his fortune on this typical tavern pastime, usually as host to his friends—the rest went into his hopeless luck at cards. We did not live in penury, however.

The guitarist produced his battered guitar, cracked here, patched there, its strings knotted over the rod which, tied to the neck, passed as a capo. He asked for a sip of wine to master his shyness, and that must have made his fingers heavy and awkward. At the first flourish, more noise than music burst from the strings and, as if it had happened yesterday, I remember my fright at this explosion of sounds, followed by tapping on the face of the broken-down instrument. I had sat down very close to him and now, rearing from the impact, I fell over backward. However, when he scratched out some of those variations he said were *soleares*, I felt them inside of me as if they had penetrated through every pore of my body.

The rapt attention with which I was following his fingers must have given him hope of ensuring his board without having to take to the road again.

"Do you want me to teach you?" he asked.

I nodded several times. In a month and a half I had learned everything the poor man knew—that is to say, very little.

"The boy has so much ability, he doesn't seem to learn but to remember what they teach him," my uncle would frequently tell his friends. I did not understand what he meant by this.

My uncle and aunt decided to take me to Granada with the kindhearted purpose of providing me with a formal education. I had just turned ten when they enrolled me at the local Institute where I was to establish a close and lasting friendship with various classmates. The most loyal, fine, and intelligent of these was Antonio Gallego Burín. Outside of the Institute I got to know Miguel Cerón, for whom I had a lifelong affection. Both now are resting in eternal peace.

3

Among the teachers under whom I studied I can only remember Teodoro Sabrás y Causapé and a Mr. Carmona. The first taught mathematics and would astonish us by the speed with which he could write figures on the blackboard and solve mathematical equations. But we hated his sarcasm and his acid tongue. He would send anyone who did not know the day's lessons to the back of the room with the most painful ridicule. Once, emphasizing his words to guarantee their sting, he asked a boy who, more because of lack of work than lack of understanding, had had to sit at the back of the room most of the term:

"Don't you feel ashamed of sitting in the dunce's seat for so long?"

"I can learn as easily from here as from up there," my classmate answered, pointing to the place of honor at the other end of the class. "I know my lessons," he added, "but what happens is that, when you ask me questions, I forget the answers."

"Leave the class at once!" shouted the teacher, raising his voice over our laughter. The boy gathered his things and left the room, whistling.

Professor Carmona was not only old and ailing, but deaf into the bargain. His geography classes were a delight to us students. Knowing he could not hear us properly, we would come up with asinine answers to his questions, which provoked bursts of laughter from the class. The game was to give as incorrect an answer as possible.

"Where does the river Guadiana rise and end?"

"In Lake Ithaca and ends in the Gulf of Mexico."

"Louder, louder!"

"In Cazorla and ends in Sanlúcar de Barrameda."

Eventually he got the right answer; we did not want to annoy him too much. Deep down we felt affection and respect for him. His kindly tolerance of our schoolboy pranks had earned him our sympathy. When at times we would exhaust his patience, he would shout an exasperated, "Order, order! I'll fail you all!" and we would fall silent and settle down, not so much out of fear of his threat but more out of consideration and regard for him.

4

The worst shouting and laughing took place when the bell rang at the end of classes announcing our freedom. We would burst out through the door of that dingy room, shouting deafeningly, into the sunny, cool street. We would then hand over our copper pennies to the limping, one-eyed wafer vendor and try our luck at his roulette wheel. Through some sleight of the old man's hands, the number of wafers we would win was never more than four. Or we would go to one of the side doors of the cathedral where a gypsy woman kept a stand and sold prickly pears. She displayed little mounds of eight or ten of the delicious fruit in front of her.

"A penny the bellyfull!" she would shout.

One day Miguel Cerón took me to the guitar workshop of Benito Ferrer, who had a large wen at the top of his head and was very skinny. As I realized much later, he was an excellent craftsman but was too poor to buy good wood. His work suffered accordingly. But now I stood transfixed by the wonders I saw. My eyes could not tire of looking at those rows of new, shining guitars hanging before me, beautiful both in form and color. Miguel made me the following proposition: he would buy one of those guitars for me, and I would repay him little by little with the pocket money my uncle gave me for the movies and for snacks. In exchange, I would give him weekly lessons and teach him all I knew about the guitar.

My aunt and uncle soon noticed I was neglecting my books and was instead spending hours glued to the guitar.

"Andresito," my uncle scolded me, "if you don't study you're going to fail this term and you'll have to take it again. We can't afford to pay twice for it. You've got to do something about that passion of yours for the guitar, boy, or—I'll do something! I'm ready to bang the thing out of commission and solve the problem once and for all."

Afraid that he might carry out his threat, I turned to Miguel who, to the great relief of both my uncle and aunt, came to take the guitar away. Peace thus returned to our home when the object distracting me from my schoolbooks was removed.

The family from the villa next door exchanged frequent visits with my uncle and aunt. They were an old couple and two daughters who were no longer young but still attractive. The youngest, Eloisa, saw my sad looks, and having learned the cause, persuaded her parents to secretly encourage and protect my love for the guitar. Since they liked to hear me play, they agreed, but only if I would promise to be a good student. They let me use a small room tucked away in the back of their house, and I kept my guitar there after I got it back from Miguel. Almost daily I would ask my uncle's permission to go to study in our neighbor's garden, saying it had nicer trees than ours. He did not always grant it, but when in his kindness he did, I would run off to seclude myself in my small paradise. It was in that happy retreat that I devoted myself to preparing my fingers by playing intricate passages. When at last I could hear the results of my slow, labored practicing, I would set the guitar down and jump for joy.

As hours would fly past without my noticing it, Eloisa took it upon herself to warn me. I would then cast a fast, all-absorbing glance at my schoolbook in case my uncle decided to question me on it, and then would rush home. Little by little Eloisa began to warn me earlier and earlier and I, little by little, began to delay my leaving. That was my first lesson in love. The teacher was over twenty and I just past twelve!

It did not take long for these and other friends, all usually older than I, to see that my devotion to the guitar went further than flamenco. One day they took me to the villa of José Gago Palomo, a colonel who had settled in the Albaicín (Granada's picturesque old section) after retiring from the army that had lost us our "Pearl of the Antilles," Cuba. There I met Gabriel Ruiz de Almodóvar who played a "good" guitar, as the flamencos have it; that is to say, he played classical music. What a wonderful discovery it was for me to hear him play one of Tárrega's preludes, even though his fingers fumbled quite often! I felt like crying, laughing, even like kissing the hands of a man who could draw such beautiful sounds from the guitar! My passion for music seemed to explode into flames. I was trembling. A sudden wave of disgust for the folk pieces I had been

6

playing came over me, mixed with a delirious obsession to learn "that music" immediately. Don Gabriel was good enough to tell my friends and me that these preludes were in print, as well as many other works by the same and other composers.

From that day on we surrendered ourselves to searching in shops, libraries and even private homes for music written for the guitar. We found some compositions by Arcas, Sor, and Giuliani, in poor and often well-worn editions. But how to read them? My knowledge of music was rudimentary. However, something of the arid lessons which the moody violinist of Villacarrillo had given me still remained in the back of my mind. I immediately got hold of a book of scales and its corresponding music theory which helped me remember the fundamentals—that is, the tone of the intervals and the time value of the notes on the staff. Of course, it was not until years later that I mastered the scales, with their changes of keys, rhythms, and values.

My friends unearthed a guitar manual of sorts, thanks to which I was able to find the notes on the instrument. Learning solfeggio that way was a herculean task. Still, I kept forging ahead, little by little. The slow progress seemed to stimulate and steel my will to overcome despair and fatigue.

Thus I began my self-education. From then on I was to be both my teacher and my pupil, in such close and enduring comradeship that, to this day, the most painful and complex events of my life succeeded only in strengthening the tie. True, in view of the unquenchable thirst for knowledge with which pupil plagued teacher, the beleaguered master seemed to offer only his fervent ignorance. In the end, however, each would forgive and understand the other.

The reader may wonder why, instead of plodding on with my lonely apprenticeship, I did not go to a teacher. The answer is quite simple. My uncle could not have spared another penny, no matter how low the fees, to pay for a teacher. Moreover, my family wouldn't have allowed me to drop out of school in order to study an instrument outside those commonly heard in concert halls—piano, violin, cello.

About those instruments. I was repelled rather than attracted to them because of the mediocre professionals who played them, in my milieu. The violinists and cellists I heard in the Granada of that time seemed to extract catlike wails from the violin and asthmatic gasps from the cello. The piano, because of its volume of sound and confusing pedal action, seemed to me like "a rectangular monster that can be made to shout by digging into its teeth," as one friend put it. But even in the hands of common people, the guitar retained that beautiful plaintive and poetic sound unmatched by any other instrument, stringed or keyboard, with the exception of the organ.

I had been captured for life by the guitar. With complete dedication, I have been totally faithful to it all my life. Faithful only to the guitar.

My first encounter with the mystery of death was when my uncle died. I still recall his face, dimly illuminated by the last radiance of life. He saw me come into the room or, rather, heard my anguished cry "Uncle Eduardo!" said from the very depths of my being, and with which I wanted to bring him back to life. I ran to bury my face in his hands and cry; he tried to comfort me in a barely audible voice. I could hardly make out his words: "It's nothing, boy, nothing. It will soon be over."

It was. He died a few hours later.

I still revere his memory today. If kindness can be taught, he had been a noble teacher. I learned a lot from his example and advice: the one always there, the other timely.

He was never harsh with me and the only punishment he ever imposed—for something I can't remember—was to tie me with a sewing thread to a bedpost.

"Heaven help you if you try to escape," he warned.

My aunt often tried his patience by making much of small domestic problems or of my pranks. She could easily break into tears of complaint. The words my uncle used to calm her were always tempered, loving and appropriate. To make us see reason, he would quote the old adage: "If your ills have no cure, why complain? If they do have a cure, why complain?"

He usually ended his gentle reprimands with a joke.

"Andresito doesn't listen to me," my aunt might complain. "All evening I've been asking him to stop humming. He knows it bothers me, but he just goes on humming. He doesn't obey me, he doesn't want to obey me!"

"My dear girl," he would tell her, "order him to hum and see how fast he obeys you!"

My grandmother, my aunt, and I moved to another villa, this one not far from the Plaza de San Nicolás, to cut down on family expenses. My window faced the Alhambra, and to its right I could see part of the city of Granada.

Granada! If in Linares I had been born into this world, it was in Granada that my eyes were opened to the beauty of life and art. The elegance and power of this Arab monument, the most glorious of all produced by that civilization, is heightened by the splendor of the surrounding nature rising in ranges of mighty mountains or sprawling out lazily into the multi-colored fusion of the *vega* plains.

The nearby Sierra Nevada stands vigil over Granada and sends down cooling breezes from its high peaks as if to temper the ardor of its sons. Rivers, streams, and small torrents flow down, carrying water from the melting snows. The Arabs knew full well how to harness that liquid treasure, not only to fertilize the soil, but to give the city a murmuring soul, that "hidden, weeping water," as the poet said. Many were the hours I spent in my youth in dreamy meditation, hearing the murmurs of the streams of the Alhambra in harmony with the rustle of the old trees of *El Bosque* and the passionate song of the nightingales!

Among Eduardo's books I found an exquisite one, Angel Ganivet's *Granada la Bella.* I devoured it at one sitting and spoke to Miguel Cerón about its graceful prose. Miguel took me to meet one of Ganivet's close relatives, a friend of his. I was so enthusiastic about the book that the family liked me at once. The daughter, Encarnación, was the prototype of the young Andalusian woman: graceful, pretty, gay, lively. She laughed melodically, almost in a descending chromatic scale. She half-closed her eyelids, with their long lashes, as she looked at the person to whom she was speaking, sending out irresistible flashes from her eyes.

I was greatly surprised when, in the course of the evening,

9

her father requested that she play the guitar. Their surprise was not less when, having listened to her with delight, I took the guitar in my arms. She had played a flamenco *granaína*. Her small fingers were nimble but weak; her tone was metallic, as though she plucked with a steel pick. But the movements of her hands—the right, rolling and thrumming, the left coaxing a vibrato—were enchanting. With its maidenly curves, the guitar was like a little girl in her arms. It was a picture worthy of Goya's brush.

They heard me play Tárrega's "Capricho Arabe," at that time the *pièce de résistance* of my repertoire and one especially suited to reach the sensitive chords of a feminine heart. The slight work, both lively and sad, did not fail to produce its effect. It cast an instant bond between Encarnación's heart and mine. Music is a swift weaver of deep feelings. As we parted that night, I pressed her hand a bit more than expected in a normal handshake. I waited. A current of fire swept up my arm as I felt her gentle response to my pressure. From that moment I swore even greater devotion to writer Ganivet.

Our romance did not go unobserved by the troubled eyes of Encarnación's mother, but the difference in our ages gave her hope that nothing too lasting was likely to come out of it.

The first words foretelling my future as an artist came from Encarnación's heart, and although I did not believe in her golden prophecies, I liked to hear them from her lips. I have always heard mysterious anticipations of my destiny from a feminine voice.

She was eight years older than I, and the vision of her image aging and of mine flourishing at the peak of life always disturbed her. That caused frequent storms in the heavens of our love, with lightning bolts of anger, menacing thunder, and squalls of tears.

I would laugh and reassure her. "You'll always be young and beautiful."

"You are making fun of my unhappy expectations," she would reply, annoyed.

Our engagement lasted two years. In the end, however, Encarnación was faced with the economic needs of her family, and we broke off. Her father had died, and the small estate he had left would provide for them for only a few months. Salvation lay in her marrying a more prosperous admirer who had been courting her for a long time.

Three nights before the wedding, I went to serenade her in a mood of sad farewell. Shortly after two in the morning, I sat by her window grille, my guitar singing in sorrow and reproach those pieces which could best express the state of my heart. When I thought I saw a shadow moving behind the glass of her windowpane and was breathlessly expecting to see Encarnación's gentle, sweet face, the figure of a sleepless man appeared at the window of the house next door. Unaware of the depth and meaning of my music, he shouted, "For heaven's sake, stop tuning that guitar and play something gay!"

From the day my uncle died, the guitar took up most of my time and my schoolbooks were almost totally neglected. My poor aunt was at the point of desperation, sure I was marked for a future without *oficio ni beneficio*, without trade or profession.

"He spends his day tiki-tik-tik plucking that guitar," she reported to the neighbors. "It's enough to drive me mad. If he loves music so much more than the career my poor Eduardo wanted for him, why not take up the violin, like that teacher in Villacarrillo, or the piano? They say that man Sarasate is a genius and that he's worshipped abroad. And what about that famous German pianist who gave that concert in Granada a while ago? What guitarist ever became famous . . . outside of a tavern?"

My aunt's distress moved me. I knew I caused it and even agreed with what she said. But my passion was greater than my love for her, stronger than my best intentions and resolve. The idea of devoting my life to the guitar professionally was not yet looming in my consciousness. In my eager devotion to it, there were no ulterior motives, no secondary considerations. I was not concerned with fame nor with what I might earn in the future from what is, today, my work.

It was pure love.

2

A FEW WEEKS AFTER Encarnación's marriage, I left Granada for my mother's home in Córdoba.

I had been brought up by my uncle Eduardo, and when I suddenly found myself face to face with the customs and habits of my mother's family, clashes were inevitable. My brother and I could not get along, and peaceful coexistence was impossible.

I decided to rent a small room on the Plaza Mayor. I furnished it sparsely with a bed, a table, and two chairs. There I took my guitar, my music and my books. I found at last the silence and peace I needed for my work.

It did not take me long to make good friends in Córdoba. Fermín Garrido, a prominent Granada doctor, had written about me to a relative, Tomás, who was an amateur guitarist and the jealous custodian of a fine collection of manuscripts, editions of Tárrega and other composers.

He generously opened up his collection to me, and thanks to him I was able to enlarge my repertoire. This, in turn, brought about new problems stemming from my scant technical knowledge.

From each difficult passage, I would extract a new study and broaden its scope to create an improved exercise. This, in turn, helped me overcome more generalized problems.

When tired of working, I would go out and walk around the city to get to know its beauty. Life seemed to have found a placid retreat for itself in Córdoba. Everything was peaceful, poetic, and profound. Except for the main ones, streets were narrow and winding. Houses leaned against each other like old women helping one another bear the weight of centuries.

Often, through the iron grilles of doorways, I would catch a glimpse of those unforgettable patios of Córdoba, filled with plants, flowers, fountains and bird songs, delicious little gardens of Paradise, at times even peopled with the houris the Prophet promised his believers.

Today, as in the days of Seneca, the people of Córdoba speak concisely, crisply. Some two thousand years ago, a true Cordovan was visited by a young Roman who talked too much about himself. The Andalusian patrician stopped him with a commanding gesture: "Silence, young man, I want to get to know you!"

Again, Guerrita, the famous Cordovan bullfighter, was once imprudently asked: "Who do you think is the best bullfighter?"

"I am the best bullfighter. After me, nobody. After nobody, Lagartijo," he said tersely, naming his closest rival.

I cannot recall which of my friends first took me to the Monserrat home. There were three sisters in the family: Elvira, Rafaela, and Laura, *in decrescendo,* according to age. The eldest taught piano at the local conservatory, the second took care of the household and, in her moments of leisure, drew exasperated complaints from a violin. Laura, the prettiest, delicate and smiling, was studying piano under her sister. Music did not awaken poetical or emotional feelings in her, although she was capable of arousing poetry in the hearts of those who gazed into her deep green eyes which glowed with a mysterious brilliance. Her lips were quick to smile between the dimples in her cheeks.

Through Laura I came to understand the type of discipline needed to study a large and complex instrument like the piano. Carefully, I would follow her fingers to discover the degree of independence, strength, and speed she developed. Back in my room I would try to apply my observations to the guitar. With indescribable joy, I found that the formulas I had worked out were helping me increase the strength, flexibility, and speed of my fingers.

At times I was so moved by those victories achieved through perseverance, that I would actually pause to thank God for His assistance.

I would like to point out to those guitarists who might be reading this that the fingering of my few diatonic scales and other exercises dates from this period, and though unpublished, they are being used by masters and students today. I have never had to change or modify them since; my experience, acquired through many years of practice, still relies on these early studies of mine. Having intuition and a will to work in the service of skill, one can find unsuspected means of shortening the rough road of apprenticeship.

Another gift I received from Laura's finely modeled hands was my first hearing of the works of Beethoven, Schumann, Chopin, Brahms, Mendelssohn. I still cherish those evenings when Laura would decipher excerpts from the masters. Her fingers grew heavy in the more difficult passages and lighter in the easier; her foot often fell asleep on the pedal and, more often than not, her reading was incorrect. This, however, did not lessen my intoxication with the music she played. I yearned for it. That music raised dreams, hopes, and desires in my soul, at once saddening and exhilarating me without my knowing why. Laura's sparkling eyes would look into mine, and then hers would cloud over when she noticed my excitement. She knew that at that moment the cause of my emotion was not her small, beautiful self; it was the poetic mystery of the music that moved me then.

14

Segovia at seventeen,
with a friend in Córdoba.

I was young and passionate; she, sweet and lovely. We became engaged. Austere Spanish tradition—disappearing today as if it were shod in seven-league boots—did not permit young lovers to see each other alone; these meetings were under the vigilant eye of a mother, an aunt, a sister, or any other person of trust, dubbed by custom as "the shotgun." The couple therefore had to refrain from expressing their desires, relying only on the passion in their eyes, on the fine shading of their voices.

Laura and I would sit quietly in the corner of the living room, whispering endearments to each other, while Rafaela read the latest afternoon news in the local paper. The only display of boldness the modest girl would permit was my taking her hand and covering it with kisses . . . when her charitable sister pretended to doze off.

The young people of today, who come so soon and so directly to sexual enjoyment, cheat themselves of the delicate pleasure and the subtle shades of eroticism which they miss by "attacking" instead of "laying siege." To reduce love to a function and that function to a minimum is gross and especially demeaning to the woman. There is wisdom in Madame Lambert's advice to the women of her time: "Modesty should be present even at the moment when one is destined to lose it."

In the months that followed, I made surprising progress. The *Método de Armonía* by the old Spanish master Hilarión Eslava fell into my hands, and I devoured it immediately. Then the problem of solitary work became more apparent. It was not always possible for me to transpose four-voices chords on the guitar, and this delayed my understanding of harmony in movement. I made titanic efforts to hear the combinations in my mind. At times I would take the guitar and try each note, one at a time, and then silently attempt to interrelate them in my mind. By doing this I was submitting my memory to an exhausting strain: imposing on it full recall of the previous notes. Exhausted, I would go to Laura and have her play them on the piano. The pleasure of hearing the pure harmony which those infernal basses produced was in itself sufficient compensation for my toil.

Another significant influence on my progress at that time

was my friendship with Luis Serrano. He was a good pianist, with a lively but undisciplined mind, witty and fun-loving. His father, a chubby little man with asthmatic breathing and strong Andalusian lisp, was a moderately accomplished organist and a modestly versed teacher of harmony. Luis would frequently replace him at one or another of his duties in the churches or schools around the city.

Luis was also my expert guide in the intricate and wondrous jungle of music. Hungry to hear it, I often went to his home when I knew I would not be interrupting his own work. Together we would run through the *Well-Tempered Clavier* and a few of the beautiful Bach choral works. His greatness overwhelmed us. It was like a gigantic tree of which some wit from Jerez, a master of Andalusian exaggeration, said, "That tree is so tall it takes two of us to look at it: when one gets tired, the other comes and goes on looking until he gets to the top!" We found Haydn clever and tender. As for Mozart, he was our Child-God. We would come back to him after any musical excursion, no matter how remote, to feast on the enchantment of his lasting grace, so attuned to our youth.

I was deeply saddened by the fact that the guitar, an instrument so rich in shading and so suited to the dreams and fantasies of a composer, should be so lacking in beautiful works such as these. It can be said that, in relation to other instruments, a guitar is what the *lied* is to opera or a quartet to an orchestra. The piano, which surpasses all other instruments in the number of works written for it, is nevertheless the most neutral. Music settles in it much as water does in a transparent, colorless crystal vessel.

In the violin, because the bow makes it possible to sustain the notes, lending them lyrical richness, the soul of music vibrates with human accents in the lower registers, while in the higher ones its sound is like glorious filaments of heavenly sounds. Think of the divinely iridescent phrase of the *andante* in Beethoven's concerto for violin and orchestra. A more sublime melody has never been structured on harmonies so inherently natural. An orchestra, due to the diversity of its instruments and its spatial goals, makes us feel as if we were witnessing the creation of a universe of sounds in which everything is disciplined, in perfect order, thanks to the magic baton of the miracle worker standing before it.

And yet, because of the richness of its tone, the guitar—and I have said this frequently—is like an orchestra seen through a pair of reversed binoculars: small, and of lyrical intimacy. In it the orchestra is refined and condensed, like a hundred forest perfumes in a small bottle.

An author friend of mine used to say blithely, "The guitar is the ideal instrument to carry on a dialogue with the woman you love. If she deceives you, use the cello to tell a friend of your sorrow and if the friend, too, betrays you, turn to the organ to tell God of your grief."

The scant repertoire of important works for the guitar compelled me to seek ways to endow the instrument with greater technical capacity, to dig a deeper and wider course so that greater streams of music could flow through it. Much of this I was to achieve years later, freeing the guitar from works written exclusively by guitarists and opening it up invitingly to good symphonic composers unfamiliar with its technique.

In Luis' home I met a young Sevillian, Rafael de Montis, who lived in Germany and who had had the good fortune to study piano under the great Eugene d'Albert. Although he undoubtedly had ability and talent, it was obvious that he lacked the patience necessary to undergo the torments of sustained and productive work. When he sat down at the piano he was whimsy personified. He never finished a piece but flitted like a butterfly over disconnected passages of technical difficulty or of deep expressive feeling, more as if to test their technical ease than to appreciate their artistic qualities. It is only fair to say, however, that his opinions on music and musicians were accepted by us as being those of an authority.

He spent a good part of the early evening correcting Luis Serrano's fingering, timing and expression, much to his father's displeasure. Mr. Serrano had been naïve enough to invite a group of musicians and family friends to meet Mr. de Montis without knowing beforehand what words of praise, if any, the young Sevillian aristocrat might have for Luis' talent. Matters turned out other than he had expected. De Montis, however, did not fail to appreciate Luis' fine artistic temperament: "You need more experience and more technical development," he said. "In any case, you still need a great teacher."

Trying to minimize the awkwardness created by de Montis' blunt advice, Luis' father pointed at me and said: "This young man plays real music on the guitar," and added lispingly, with a double-edged smile, "nothing less than Chopin preludes and mazurkas and short pieces by Schumann and Mendelssohn. He'll even take on Bach!"

Aware of his father's intention, Luis, who liked me, replied with serious enthusiasm: "Those single pieces are beautiful on the guitar, and Andrés plays them with the greatest taste."

Without further hesitation, Luis went into his room and brought out a guitar. I need not describe my obstinate resistance to play. I felt depressed and wanted to sneak away. The company insisted, some with a touch of sarcasm. Luis persisted in good faith. Mr. de Montis was silent.

I was careful not to choose any of the pieces mentioned by Luis' father, all of which were written for the piano and would have subjected me to even greater disparagement than that inflicted on the son. I began with a study in B minor by Sor, followed by a short prelude by Tárrega and his *arpeggio* study in A major. Then I paused for breath. Rafael de Montis' expression was one of pleased surprise. "Good, young man, good!"

I believed that de Montis, accustomed to the harsh sound of the flamenco guitar, its riotous fingering and steel-like improvisations, had been favorably impressed by the sweet tone of its soft voice as it sang melodiously, backed by varied and logical harmony.

"Play some of those pieces Mr. Serrano mentioned," he asked me in a moment.

Trembling, barely able to control my fingers, I played Tárrega's transcription of the Bach *bourrée* in B minor from the second sonata for solo violin. I finished it and was unhappy with myself. "If you will allow me, I'll play it again."

Without waiting for an answer, I played it through again, this time cleanly. Rafael de Montis was smiling.

"Have you played in public?" he asked.

"Oh, no sir!" I exclaimed and added, "Some friends in Granada have asked me to play in the Arts Center there, and I'm now working on the program."

"Go to Granada and then come on to Seville and look for me," he said, to everyone's great surprise.

Rafael de Montis' words kept me awake many a night. Except for Laura and Luis, those who had heard me play in Granada and Córdoba were people whose musical opinion was not highly qualified. Thus I was profoundly touched when someone as expert in judging the talent of famous foreign artists as Mr. de Montis should have expressed a favorable opinion about a poor upstart like me, especially without disparaging the guitar as an instrument.

Confidence, on which commitment must draw if it is to show results, rose from the very depth of my being.

I was sixteen or seventeen years old. I gave up my secondary school studies and wrote to Miguel Cerón, asking him to organize the recital in the Granada Arts Center. A date toward the end of 1909 was chosen for the concert and, the day after the first public performance in my life, a moderately favorable review, written by Alberto Alvarez Cienfuegos, appeared in the *Noticiero Granadino*. Reading it, I saw myself as world-famous. Suddenly I decided to be the Apostle of the guitar.

I set out with a firm stride.

3

SHORTLY AFTER MY GRANADA CONCERT I returned to Córdoba and, within two weeks, went on to Seville. Laura wanted to come with me but was deterred by my irrefutable arguments and her good sense. For her, the goal of our flight was an early marriage: we were to beat a direct path to the church, while I was worried by the fact that the audience at the Arts Center in Granada might have been too partisan, that its kind acclaim was little else than a show of sympathy for a youngster they all knew and whom the majority considered a friend. I was already tantalized, too, by the idea of facing the cold appraisal of an unknown audience without any previous ties to me, one whose response would be both objective and spontaneous. Remembering the offer of Rafael de Montis, the young Sevillian pianist, I went to Seville.

Rafael lived up to his promise and begrudged me no effort. He invited to his home the cream of Seville's musical world and some of his aristocratic circle who, though not very musically inclined, were friends. I played . . . I played with the fervor of an inexperienced artist, anxious to earn for himself —and in this case, for his instrument as well—hearts rather than praise. Father Torres, the cathedral's choirmaster, "legitimized" the approval of all those present. They offered to cooperate in organizing public and private concerts from which I could reap some benefit—something I badly needed.

Visibly moved, old Dr. Sánchez Cid, a lifelong champion and member of the guitar establishment, came up to congratulate me. He had fought many a fierce battle for the guitar without making many converts among the skeptical music lovers who, in deference to him, attended his gatherings. When he tried to display the guitar's beauty, his fingers failed him and he made such unforgivable mistakes, even in the easiest passages, that his friends ended up laughing at his efforts and attributing to the guitar flaws which sprang solely from the good doctor's lack of dexterity.

"Now those unbelievers will see how right I was!" he assured me. Lowering his voice, he continued, "I have heart trouble. If the joy I have felt hearing you tonight should shorten my life, then praised be God!"

The *soirée* at Rafael de Montis' home ended very late. When I went to get my coat, I found a beautiful carnation pinned to the lapel. It had been placed there by Maria, Rafael's younger sister. It was her sign of applause.

I hid my surprise, suspecting that whoever had put it there would be watching nearby and would appreciate my discretion. While in Córdoba, Rafael had spoken much about his family: his mother, an invalid, and his two sisters. Lucita, the elder, was pretty, serious, reasonable, and quiet, he said, while Maria was beautiful, lively, whimsical, and witty. I thought of her when I saw the carnation.

When I went back to their house for lunch the next day, she said, "My brother spoke so much of you that he bored me and made me dislike you. That's why I didn't want to sit in the living room last night. But I listened to you from the next room in the dark."

One must believe in love at first sight. At least, no time is lost that way; that is certain. I was immediately bewitched by the impishness of her Sevillian face, by the ease and chimes of her laughter, by her typically Andalusian banter. "Looking at you," I mused, "I seem to remember a folk ballad that could have been inspired by you."

"Well? Go on, let me hear it."

¿Con qué te lavas la cara	With what do you bathe your face?
que tan rebonita estás?	You look so very pretty
Me lavo con agua clara	I bathe it with clear water
y . . . Dios pone lo demás.	And . . . then God adds the rest.

"You flatterer! It's beautiful, as if it had come from your guitar."

From my first visit to the de Montis home, I became a friend of Miguel Angel del Pino. He blamed his parents for his name, Michelangelo, which he found extravagant, as he was a painter himself. Jokingly, he said that if his name went down in the history of art it would be as Michelangelo *Malarroti*—as against the great master's surname, *Buonarroti*. Gustavo Bacarisas, notwithstanding the considerable difference in our age, also made me feel I was an old comrade from the start. I would often go to the *Casa de los Estudios* to see my friends there, all painters, young and old, who had their studios in the *Casa*; some were known not only in Seville but throughout Spain and even abroad. It was there that Gómez Gil painted seascapes and it was rumored that for him to capture the feel of the waves, one of his students would stir up a storm in a pail of water! Also Rico Cejudo, who deftly hummed flamenco *seguiriyas*, *soleares*, and *tarantas* in excellent style which made us sit and listen quietly. The gracious Count of Aguiar had a studio in the *Casa* as did, if my memory does not fail me, the haughty and stern Gonzalo Bilbao. The younger men, Martínez, Grosso and del Pino himself, were developing their different skills there, all lively and warmhearted young fellows.

Miguel Angel del Pino flattered me by wanting to do my

portrait playing the guitar, but as I had never posed before, each session turned into long, bitter hours for us both. The absolute stillness he required of me made my features lose their natural expression, which irritated him. Then, forgetting I was posing, I would start playing; this also annoyed him. To prevent his invective and my retorts from getting too heated, we postponed the project till later; this turned out to be in 1926, when we were both living in Paris. It is one of the best portraits to come from his brush and, without doubt, the best any artist has been able to do of me.

In Miguel Angel I found both regard and support. Our friendship developed smoothly and was to last, unspoiled, for all the years to come. Since those delightful days in Seville, we have shared sorrow and glory in Madrid, Paris, Rome, Buenos Aires, and Montevideo. If I did not follow his excellent advice in artistic or sentimental matters, it is because I am like that sly *Granadino* whose stock answer to his counselors was: "Please excuse me if I do not follow your advice. I prefer to make my own mistakes!"

Gustavo Bacarisas also worked at the *Casa*. He was a perfect gentleman and most certainly no romantic bore. His art was very "private"; he was an artist only within the four walls of his studio. Excellently dressed, always moderate in gesture, deferential and pleasant in conversation, he was ever kind to his juniors. Without causing any offense, he maintained a certain calculated distance, halfway between what could have seemed like discourteous aloofness or an overbearing presence. He was not very tall, somewhat heavy, but good-looking.

Both he and his work impressed me very much. At that time he was finishing his painting, *La Soleá*, a scene of an al fresco fiesta in Seville. The soft gamut of lights with which he so poetically sheathed the central feminine figure appeared to come from a source more ethereal, less physical, than the burning, dazzling sun of Seville. It was said that Gustavo had been in love with "La Soleá," a gypsy girl from the Macarena quarter, beautiful, graceful, melancholic, in whose eyes flashed the wisdom of centuries. That magnificent painting can be seen today in the Museum of Seville.

One night Gustavo asked me to bring my guitar to his studio; he wanted to increase the number of my followers before my first concert was announced. Many of his friends were there. The Argentines Roberto Lavilier and Rodolfo Franco, the former a diplomat and the latter a painter; Luis Bagaria, witty and popular, in spite or because of his marked Catalan accent—a formal kind of speech which is less welcome in Seville than elsewhere in the Peninsula. Such was the local feeling that there is a story about an Andalusian husband who returns home in the evening to greet his wife with a kiss and a strangely correct "Good evening, my dear." The wife, who is reputed to have a keen ear for Spanish regional accents, exclaims immediately, "You've been talking with a Catalan!"

The Moorish poet José Muñoz San Román, an inveterate procrastinator, was also present as was the popular singer, Tórtola Valencia, then silm, attractive, and picturesque. Dr. Sánchez Cid came to hear me again, against his doctor's orders and behaving like a disobedient little boy. Juanito Lafita, who managed somehow to be everywhere. Also the poet Juan Ramón Jiménez, with his sad, large expressive eyes and thick beard, his soft, curt laugh, so very short that his features would settle back instantly into his unfailing expression of tranquil, poetic melancholy. And, of course, del Pino and other friends from the *Casa de los Estudios*. Rafael de Montis was not in Seville that day.

Being among so many artists made me shy. Prudence, I decided, indicated I stay in the background. I would look and listen . . . until they asked my to play.

Gustavo served a full-bodied Moriles wine which helped add fuel to his gathering and loosened everybody's tongue.

Tórtola Valencia's extravagant behavior made me uneasy. She was bold and aggressive. Speaking in a mixture of Spanish and English, according to Rodolfo Franco she was crude in both tongues, using words culled from the docks of both the Guadalquivir and the Thames. Although Rodolfo was paying her close court, she appeared to be obsessed by Bagaria.

"Listen, clown, if you ridicule me in one of those sketches that make people laugh, I'll cut you down to size and won't go with you tonight. Think it over," she shouted at him in English.

Bagaria continued his drawing without paying attention.

"With that beautiful head of yours, you could do wonderful things. As it is, you're nothing but a buffoon with a crayon," she added.

"Lafita," del Pino interrupted. "Is it true that you sent a birthday card to your parents on your birthday, congratulating them for having had the honor of bringing you into this world?"

"What's wrong, San Román," Lafita called across the room. "Why so silent and pensive?"

"I was tired when I got up."

"Maybe you dreamt you had been working!"

"You're not always as funny as you think, Lafita."

These and other quips were thrown about the room, but then suddenly voices would drop.

"Some times, when you go to see him," somebody said, speaking of Juan Ramón Jiménez's obsession with silence, "the person who opens the door puts a finger to his lips and signals with his eyes to the second floor, pleading, 'Please, please, don't make any noise. Juan Ramón is having a poem.' "

The disjointed chatter, the jokes and laughter, Tórtola's impudence, the whole frivolous air of the party, made me unwilling to play. I wanted to suggest to Gustavo that we postpone the music and I got up to tell him this, but he guessed immediately what was on my mind. He put his fingers between his lips and called for silence.

"Friends, I asked you here tonight to listen to a young artist who is beginning his career," he told them. "Because he has been brave enough to choose an instrument with little musical repute, it is going to be difficult for him to be successful. I ask for your attention so you can hear him . . . and a little generosity, so you can help him."

All eyes turned to me, increasing my shyness.

"I don't want to be a wet blanket," I told them. "I'll play some other time, if you like."

I did play, and having heard me that night, many of the listeners became twofold friends: friends of the guitar and

26

friends of mine. Roberto Lavilier, the Argentinian writer-diplo-mat whom Gustavo brought, expressed his surprise at hearing classical music played on this instrument.

"Argentina is the second homeland of the guitar, even if we don't play it in the same artistic vein you do. I'm sure you'll be most welcome there. Don't put off going to my country. You can count on me to help you get your visa and to introduce you to friends who can be of help to you over there."

I was in Seville for over a year, a captive of Maria de Montis' dark eyes. I went in and out of her house as if it were my home. Her mother took kindly to me, and Lucita, her sister, pretended to ignore our courtship. Although we were not formally engaged, "Mariquilla" was the delightful tyrant of my life. She demanded that I study in her presence and thus inhibited my practicing. She often made me stay for lunch or dinner. Aware of my friendship with Miguel Angel del Pino and Bacarisas and of the pleasure their companionship gave me, she went so far as to persuade her mother to have Miguel paint her portrait: I would not have to leave *her* to see *him*. While she posed for the portrait, we chatted in the room which had been chosen as a studio. Bacarisas, Father Torres, Juan Lafita, Dr. Sánchez Cid and others were there daily and often insisted that I play background music for Miguel's brush just as once some lute player might have performed for Tintoretto. Although in the end Miguel was not able to catch Maria's ex-pressive vitality, I was glad the commission had fallen to him. Since his father's death, he had heroically supported his mother and two sisters, solely by his painting. His younger brother had shirked any such obligation and gone off to Argentina, ending up by making a very advantageous marriage in Buenos Aires, and still not helping his family in Seville. This responsibility he left to Miguel.

After playing in Rafael de Montis' home and in Baca-risas' studio I gave a presentation concert in the *Ateneo* and more than fifteen public and private recitals in theaters, clubs, and private homes, and was rewarded more generously than a beginning artist deserved. With money in my pocket and such excellent friends about me, I was in the best of all possible worlds. Poets sang my praises in verse . . . and women smiled on me!

My youthful desire to wander the world dozed off in the beloved lap of Seville at this first joyful budding of my fame. It was the Sevillians themselves who punished me for remaining there as long as I did. But this is in the natural order of things: an artist should vanish once his mission is completed. He should be seen by his admirers, but only briefly, and at very long intervals.

Wandering companions in the arts: never let your pilgrimage come to a halt in any city, however attractive or propitious the stop may seem, unless you feel the urge to build your nest there! If you decide to stay and become just another resident, forget the audience that sang your praises when you first arrived and do not seek it out anew, lest you suffer bitter disillusionment. Remember what happened to the famous poet José Zorilla in Granada when that city crowned him and its plazas blazed with festivals in his honor! Bedazzled by the many laurels showered on him by the generous *Granadinos*, he put off departure several times. O, perverse fate! There began to appear in large letters on the walls of the city streets the plea: "Bard, depart!"

After allowing my audience to rest for fourteen months, I decided to gather it about me once again. It came to neither of the two concerts I gave. At the first one there were a few friends . . . but even they were not present at the second.

"Nobody went to Andrés' first concert and fewer went to the second," was the way Lafita, always ready with a joke, put it.

Not wishing to see me return to Córdoba downcast, my Sevillian friends sent me off to other Andalusian cities, Huelva, Cádiz, and Jerez, well provided with impressive letters of introduction. My concert in Huelva was nearly a private one: the small salon of the clubhouse where I played was almost deserted. A decrepit old man snored; another read the newspaper. Six or seven listened, expressing contempt, or entirely indifferent to my music. One of them, taken by the rhythm of a dance, followed what he imagined to be the beat with his foot and his hands. I finally gave up and left. At the door, the concierge handed me a small envelope in which I found ten *duros* —fifty *pesetas!*

In Cádiz, Francisco García Arboleya and writer Alfonso Hernández Catá, the Cuban consul in Cádiz, arranged two public concerts, but expenses wiped out the box-office gross, much to their disappointment.

A novitiate in the arts is fraught with hurdles, but how little do these discourage the young artist!

I spent fifteen days in Jerez, and this noble city opened its doors to me more cordially. Luis Pérez Lila, in his generous efforts to introduce me to as many of his friends in as little time as possible, took me on a whirlwind tour of private homes, bars, tearooms, even distant country estates. Between public and private recitals, I was able to put aside some five hundred *pesetas,* a fabulous amount for the young boy that I was! With this financial respite and full of hope, I started back to Seville, promising myself I would not put off my departure for Madrid, the goal of my life at that time.

I returned to Seville and once again beheld the cathedral, smiled at the tower of the Giralda, bathed my soul in the silence of the *Plaza de Santa Cruz*. Strolling along the banks of the Guadalquivir, these verses of Lope de Vega came to my mind:

¡Oh río de Sevilla,	O, river of Seville,
qué bien pareces	how beautiful you seem
lleno de velas blancas	in sails of white
y palos verdes!	and masts of green!

I had told Maria de Montis I would see her at sunset and finally turned my steps to the street of Conde de Tojar, where the family lived. Approaching the grilled window which, like a small garden, was overflowing with plants and flowers, I saw Maria's small face among them. At first sight, I noticed her forehead furrowed. Her mood, usually so radiantly happy, was subdued that evening.

"What is it, Maria?" I asked. "Worry changes your face so, I thought I was at the wrong window."

"When are you leaving again?" she immediately asked.

"Tomorrow. I'm stopping off in Córdoba and then going on to Madrid." I hesitated, then continued. "Maria, it's terribly difficult to leave you and Seville, but I must make that sacrifice. There's nothing left for me to do here. The public has turned its back on me, and there is little point in trying to win it back. Madrid is the center of the arts in Spain, and I have to earn my spurs there. With God's help, if I can persuade the Madrid critics and music lovers to listen to me, then the provincial cities will accept me, and my position will change."

"Please stay, Andrés. Don't go!" Her voice trembled and her fluttering eyes moistened. "The letters I have received from you during your increasing travels caused me more sorrow than pleasure, they seemed to come from so far away . . . and yet you were so close. I read them aloud over and over but found myself getting angry at my own voice. Yes, yes, I learned from them that I am not the most vital concern of your heart. Your endearing words were not lies, but they sounded like a *campana rajá,* a cracked bell. How happy you sounded, telling me of your success, of some favorable comment in the paper, or describing the people you met, or your impressions of the cities you visited. Your loving little words were there . . . but only as strangers, like country folk in a big city.

"I know there is no other woman; my heart tells me so. It's what you call your art. For me it is only an excuse, an excuse to wander the world looking for success . . . because, without ever leaving my side you could become as great an artist as anyone. Don't go, Andresillo! My people can help you find a regular job—you'll have enough to live on. When we're more mature, in two or three years, we can get married. Forget about traveling around the world with your guitar: you'll be able to play in our own little house and no one, no one will reward you more than I."

Tenderly I tried to persuade her that both things were possible, that there was no contradiction between our love and my art, that as the old folk ballad goes:

La ausencia es como el aire,	Absence is like air,
que apaga fuego chico	It smothers little flames
y enciende el grande.	And feeds great fires.

30

"Perhaps I love you more than you love me," I told her. "I'm sure we can be happy, not by planting our roots in home soil, but by spreading our wings. A regular job! We artists are good for no other job than the hard work to which we have been sentenced by our art. We are born to the fate of being poets, painters, or musicians, and if we try to change it, we are lost men. Instead of becoming a slave to a job at which I could never be any good and for which I have no inclination, I am going to devote these years of waiting to perfecting my art and with the help of Heaven, to making my name known and loved. Then I'll come to get you, Maria. Together we'll fly to the four corners of the earth!"

"You don't love me, you don't love me," she cried out.

Suddenly, as if realizing the full strength of my decision, her attitude and tone changed. Biting the words with anger, she hurled this gypsy curse at me before she slammed the window shut: "*¡Ojalá te quedes manco!*"

She had wished me the loss of my hands.

I left Seville the next day. He who has not lived in that charming city of Andalusian grace, or never had a love there, will find it difficult to understand how heartrending it is to leave Seville.

Sixty-odd years have passed and, to this day, a misty sadness overcomes me when I recall my leaving. I wrote to her, but my letters had no response. I asked friends to intercede, but there were no answers to my messages, no signs of hope.

Seeking refuge, I submerged myself in my studies, making them my very life and finally finding consolation and peace in them. The sorrows sown by life blossom in the heart of the artist in time and saturate his work with strong perfume. "The poet need not weep . . . but he has to have wept," said an Andalusian bard.

It was Maria who made me understand the finer shades of beauty and, perhaps, also helped me to express them.

THE COST OF LIVING in Madrid was going to be substantially higher than in Seville so, to cover my expenses for the first few months there, I decided to enlarge my nest egg with the receipts from one or two concerts in Córdoba. I asked the opinion of my friends, José Chacón, the son of the military governor, Pedro Antonio Baquerizo, Luis Serrano, and others. They nurtured my hopes enthusiastically and immediately distributed among themselves the various tasks the concerts involved. After much thought was given as to where the concerts should be given, it was decided that the auditorium of the conservatory was the most appropriate place and Baquerizo was put in charge of making that arrangement. José Chacón took on the task of advertising in the local press and having wall-posters put up. Luis Serrano was to induce the local aficionados to grant me the honor of attending, once they stopped off at the box office, of course. Another friend, a soldier, undertook a campaign among members of the local garrison. Skeptical and nervous, I undertook the chore of waiting.

The occasion did not seem unfavorable. Reports which had appeared in the Seville, Granada, and Cádiz press had been picked up by the Córdoba papers and apparently had tempered many of the guitar's revilers. The public has a tendency to let its opinions be swayed by the somewhat erratic criteria of the press, although it may recognize the ease with which it, the press, espouses and then abandons causes, excites and then dampens passions, and *"face a los omes e las gasta,"* or makes and breaks men, if you will pardon my early Castilian. Many a Cordovan, once a sworn enemy of the concert guitar, now suddenly found it to be a most suitable vehicle for classical music; indeed, for anything classical—including, possibly, classical Greek drama were the press to suggest such a thing.

However, at that time I had a formidable detractor of my instrument in José Fernández Bordas. His antagonism and that of his brother Antonio, the violinist, created many problems for me. He would wince with displeasure whenever my name was mentioned, and he disparaged the guitar at every opportunity. His negative attitude seriously obstructed my career as a young musician, influencing musical organizations to turn a deaf ear to my work and closing their doors to me—just when I most needed to work in order to make even a modest living.

Small, plump Don José had a high-pitched, almost effeminate voice which contrasted markedly with his bushy graying beard. He worked at the Real Estate Tax Bureau and sought relief from his tedious job in the pleasures of the piano. He had been unable to master the complexities of musical execution, and so had turned to musicology—a frequent alternative of those whom the capricious deity has not treated very kindly. Even so, at most, Don José had only managed to get his foot in the temple's door; he stopped at the threshold, just this side of research, limiting himself to presenting secondhand facts at his fashionable lectures.

A sharp-tongued journalist who got bored at one of those

elegant lectures and left early, met a good friend of Don José's who was arriving late.

"Has he finished?" the friend asked.

"Yes, long ago, but he's still talking," replied the journalist.

And so, my friend Baquerizo went to request the concert hall for my projected recital. Don José, whose opinion was highly regarded by the amiable director of the conservatory, Cipriano Martínez Ruckert, vigorously expressed his opposition.

"Besides," he added, "Alfred Cortot, the French pianist, and my brother Antonio, are on a concert tour of Spain and will soon be granting the conservatory the honor of performing there," he said. "Do you think it proper that such an out-standing event should be preceded by another of such questionable artistic value?"

Baquerizo dared to raise his voice on my behalf. "But Don José, Andrés has played in Granada, Seville, Huelva, and Cádiz. The papers have been full of praises and testify to the high standard of his work."

"High standard! Stuff and nonsense, man! How can anyone put up with a mere boy who besides is doing so much harm to music? Schumann, Chopin, Mendelssohn, dressed up in fla-menco trappings! And who are those you say are being so generous with their praise? Journalists with no musical back-ground, social columnists, third-rate poets! For God's sake, man!"

This was the straw that broke the camel's back. My plans and hopes had stumbled on Don José, and that was that. My four musketeers had their hands tied, and I couldn't wait to leave town.

Fate, however, had plans of its own, as I am most happy and grateful to report. Don Fernando Barba and his sweet, charming wife, both great lovers of music, treated me with open sympathy and even seemed to be pleased when my friend Luis Serrano would insist that I play for them. Don Fernando felt that I put the guitar out of kilter, but held out the hope that I would regain my sanity and take up the cello, foreseeing a reasonably secure future for me if I followed his advice.

Luis explained to him why my plans for the Córdoba con-certs had been thwarted.

Regretting Don José's antagonism toward me, Fernando Barba asked Luis to come to see him the next morning. That morning, he gave Luis an envelope for me containing two hundred *pesetas* and a short note wishing me well in Madrid. He also begged Luis to be very tactful when handing the gift over to me. Luis handled his mission well. I surrendered to his arguments, agreeing that to return the generous and opportune present would be to repay a very thoughtful gesture with uncalled-for pride.

A few days later, Alfred Cortot and Antonio Fernández Bordas arrived in Córdoba to give their concert at the conservatory. That concert was my first religious experience with music as a member of an audience. When I later told Cortot of this, we agreed that, from then on, he was to call me *mon filleul*, my godson, and I was to call him *mon parrain*, my godfather.

Cortot immediately captivated the audience. At the time he wore his long black hair hanging over the right side of his face, as if the explosion of his abundant mane were a reflection of his formidable talent.

I still remember vividly the energy, mixed with fleeting tenderness, with which he played Liszt's *St. Francis de Paul Walking on the Waters*. The somber beautiful song which is the theme of the work, sustained at times by firm solid chords, at others by fighting the surging waves of scales and arpeggios, roused echoes in the soul; I was still new to such musical emotions. The miracle of the saint's steps on the waters appeared trivial compared to the wonder of sound created by a great pianist. He carried everything before him, including his audience in Córdoba.

If the fascinated listeners did not weary of applauding the French pianist, their enthusiasm did not overflow when it came to Antonio Fernández Bordas. No one has ever denied that his musical talents were less imposing than his undoubted ability as a school administrator. Thus, when disillusionment had clipped his wings as a virtuoso, he went to roost at the Madrid Conservatory and contrived, within a very short time, to build a nest in the director's chair. From then on his musical soul was muted.

On the eve of my departure for Madrid my friends invited me to have a few drinks of manzanilla, the sharp dry sherry, at Don Paco's tavern, one of the most typical in Córdoba. A narrow alley led to it: a large patio edged with Spanish tiles. The walls were covered with fading bullfight posters recalling brave performances of the past whose memory Don Paco kept alive for the delight of old aficionados and the edification of young ones. Bold and lively, Don Paco smiled at friends and acquaintances from his command post at the bar, or wove his way between the tables, breaking here and there into a conversation with ease wit and tact, stopping to drop an opportune comment or *bon mot* as he passed a group of regular guests.

Bottles of wine and liquor lined the heavy shelving behind the bar. Above, presiding in the center from a vaulted niche, there was the powerful mounted head of a Miura bull killed years back by the great Lagartijo. A metal plaque below gave the date of the memorable fight, the bull's lineage, a brief account of his courageous performance in the ring, and other important dctails of the historic event.

The manzanilla soon sent our blood racing and we asked for its complement: music and song—or, as they call it in Andalusia, *toque y cante*. The Croesus hosting our group was Pedro Antonio Baquerizo, and he summoned the famous flamenco singer, El Niño de Jerez, and the equally celebrated guitarist, Miguel Borrull. I begged my companions not to reveal my connection with the guitar.

El Niño de Jerez came in and stood looking down on us, majestic as a pharaoh.

"I might as well warn you, fellows," he said. "I don't sing just to amuse strangers to the art. I sing only to make others suffer with me."

With a solemn, thoughtful *olé* of approval, his companion Borrull backed him up, while we looked at them in almost frightened silence. As a token of conciliation, one of our group, Moisés, borrowed Borrull's guitar and wove some gypsy *seguiriya* variations, not very skillfully, but with style and feeling.

"Ah, that's different," El Niño approved. "If it's not a

drinking spree that you want, I'm with you," and, nodding to Borrull, he added, "Let's go!"

He cleared his marvelous throat, washed it down with a formidable gulp of manzanilla, and tipped his wide-brimmed Córdoba hat forward, leaving it slightly askew on his head. As if to give us a prelude of the anguish he was about to depict in song, he held out his clawlike hand to us. There was the customary introduction and the *copla* surged magnificently from the lament of a *soleá:*

A mi puerta has de llamar	I won't open my door
y no te he de bajar a abrir	when you come calling
y me has de sentir llorar.	but I'll cry behind it.

A fervent *olé* rose from all of us. The guitarist, in noble contest with his fellow artist, played deftly with a variety of shadings; now reconciling the rhythm to the song's deep voices, now vying with them, with precision and gusto; alternating the rolling of his fingers on the strings with sharp taps of percussion on the guitar's face, or muting it with the palm of his hand, to fall suddenly silent, and . . . surge again with resonant power. When the last sigh of the ballad seemed to die away in the throat of the singer, the guitarist so lowered the strength of his *rasgueado* that the accompaniment turned into a background of distant murmurs. Little by little, following the song, the sound increased until it reached a conclusion of frenzied rolling which seemed to break up the melancholy voice of the guitar into a thousand particles of sound.

"Young man, do you play guitar?" Miguel Borrull asked, suddenly turning to me. Apparently he noticed with suspicion my interest in his performance. He was afraid I might be stealing some of his variations.

"A little," I answered, "but I wouldn't even dare tune a guitar in the presence of my master, Andrés Segovia." I pointed to Roberto Ramaugé, an Argentine painter who was also a lazy amateur and could pick a few simple tunes.

Borrull stood up to greet him deferentially, while we tried to hide our smiles.

"I have heard your name praised; it is an honor to meet

37

you," the guitarist exclaimed, "but I was told you were from *Graná*; from the few words you have spoken here I would say you were from America. Some good bullfighters come from Mexico—why shouldn't good guitarists come from around there, too." Handing the instrument to Ramaugé, he added, "This is what they call a rare pearl. Manuel Ramírez made it."

Embarrassed, Ramaugé looked around at us.

"Please forgive us, Miguel," I broke in. "The master plays by music, not by ear; and since some of your strings have been tied over the capo, he couldn't play on the full extent of the fingerboard. I'll make an effort to control my shyness. Let me play something he has taught me, if you will excuse my lack of skill. I'll be nothing but the shadow of the master but. . . ."

"Play if you must," was Borrull's cold reply.

Taking the guitar in my arms I played a fast succession of arpeggios and scales to warm up. Borrull turned to stare at Ramaugé and, raising his hands to his head, cried out:

"Jesus, how the master must play!"

Had I been Orpheus himself and performed marvels with my fingers, wringing the very soul out of that guitar, Miguel would not have been impressed. With each difficult passage that I executed adroitly, with each melodic phrase I wrested deliberately to move him, he repeated vehemently his praise for the supposed Andrés Segovia. Several times he interrupted me to take the instrument away and offer it to Ramaugé who, encouraged by wine, having never been the subject of such persistent attention and requests to display his talents, was on the point of letting the cat out of the bag by actually playing. My obvious resolve not to let Ramaugé do so annoyed Borrull.

"Listen, fellow," he snapped, "when there's a captain on the bridge, sailors don't issue orders. God first and then His angels. You follow me?"

Realizing he might be extremely offended should we tell him the truth, we asked El Niño to make us "suffer" with another of his devastating *coplas*. A long time later, after more than a dozen bottles of wine had been consumed, we got up to go. Pedro Antonio settled up with these outstanding artists, and we started for the door. Passing the bar we overheard Eduardo

Jover expounding, as usual, against flamenco, any and all things flamenco.

"This bloody drama of the bullring will ruin Spain! Our arts and sciences are languishing. Bullfighters Guerra and Lagartijo are idolized while Echegaray and other great writers are ignored." Pointing to the head of the Miura bull in its niche, his anger against bullfighting exploded: "Isn't it shameful to see that head there?"

Don Paco slyly interjected, "Instead of playwright Benavente's?"

5

I TOOK THE MAIL TRAIN to Madrid; it was less expensive than the express.

My small suitcase held more books and sheet music than clothes, and in an older, frayed-looking satchel I had a mixed bag of lunch and shaving things; these, and my guitar in its case, were really all I owned in the world.

Here!'' shouted the porter carrying my bags, and I climbed up into the second-class compartment he indicated. I myself placed my guitar case in the safest nook I could find, while the porter stuffed my other belongings among the baggage already on the overloaded rack. I sat down and looked about at my traveling companions.

The first one I inspected was a shapeless, heavy-set man with a narrow, wrinkled forehead, bushy eyebrows and the fierce, close-set eyes of a wild boar. He had a big nose with flaring nostrils through which the air seemed to whistle as it passed through; his puffy, insolent lips had a disdainful twist to them; his ears were big, hairy, red, like repugnant insects. I turned my gaze from this disagreeable creature to the beautiful face of a young girl who was obviously traveling with an older woman—the kind who tries to hide her age—and a delicate-looking man who had the appearance of having aged prematurely due to a long illness. This poor man's misty gaze was not fixed on the surroundings, nor was it turned inwards on an inner world; it seemed to be submerged in a thick mental fog. The girl clearly was embarrassed by the soft but full curves beginning to show in her small, graceful body. She had a fine and beautiful face, however, highlighted by large blue eyes under her perfectly arched forehead. I made myself a mental note to continue observing her later and turned to examine the last two occupants of the compartment: a frankly fat priest, who was apparently content to move through life taxing the earth with a bodily weight which might endanger his rewards in Heaven. He had in his care a lively boy whom the reverend scolded continuously in a low voice, in the forlorn hope of curbing his childish restlessness.

The train started with a creak and began to move slowly. It is said that outside of Spain travelers can spend days together and address each other only in the most dire necessity. Spaniards are fond of telling a story about an Italian, traveling in the United States, who attempts to start a conversation with his neighbor.

"It's a nice day," he says tentatively.

Annoyed by this display of foreign boldness, the American answers aggressively, "Who said it wasn't?" and turns his back on the Italian.

Such aloofness is not possible in Spain. The closed compartments of the trains in those days became convivial centers of conversation. On reaching their destination, passengers who had spent so many long hours together bid each other farewell like lifelong friends, or, if they had been irritated by some heated argument, parting is the time to make solemn promises to crack the skull of the other at the first available opportunity.

"Is it a child's body you've got in that box?" asked the

man who looked like a wild boar, pointing at the guitar case, which actually did bear some resemblance to a small coffin.

"God protect us!" exclaimed the priest.

"There is nothing to worry about," I assured the company. "It's a guitar. I prefer to keep it in a case which doesn't quite reveal its contents."

"But it doesn't make sense," said the girl, "to put such a gay instrument in such a sad-looking case!"

"So, just as I suspected, we've got one of those who play from sheet music," said the man with the thick eyebrows, accenting his sneer, if such a thing were possible.

"A barber friend of mine also plays prissy polkas and waltzes on the guitar. I tell him he's been pawing men's cheeks so long that he's becoming a queer. What good is a guitar without singing and dancing, without women and wine?"

He looked around, seeking the others' approval.

"You're wrong," the priest disagreed. "I've heard Julian Arcas play, and it was as if celestial music had descended on us. It was astonishing, too, how he could imitate a scolding old man or a young girl at her prayers. It was really amazing!"

"People in general turn to the guitar," I said, addressing the girl in particular, "because no other instrument available to all offers an easier background of harmony to accompany folk song or popular music. Anyone without training can pick a tune on it. And besides it weighs so little! The Spanish soldier, 'he who has felt the curve of the earth under his feet,' as the saying goes, took it with him wherever he went, and so the guitar became native to the most remote places of the world. Also, its sound is sad; it echoes the song in man's soul, inviting him to make it his companion. Still, it would be unfair to limit the beauty of this instrument to the mere accompaniment of folk song and dances," I added for the benefit of the wild boar, "or to confine it," this for the priest, "to the elemental kind of music Julian Arcas played. Don Julian was a spontaneous artist, not a cultivated one. The scope of the guitar has to be widened, music of greater significance should be played on it, such as Fernando Sor, Mauro Giuliani or Francisco Tárrega, wrote for it."

While I was thus carried away the barber's friend took

42

from his knapsack a formidable onion and half a loaf of appetizing dark bread. He opened one of those large Albacete switchblade knives which make your blood run cold when some barbarian displays it and makes its springs creak. He began cutting large slices of bread and onion, eating them with obvious and slow relish. The wine he poured from a leather *bota* went down his throat with a gurgling, repulsive sound.

"Ha! I was right!" he exclaimed, wiping his mouth with the back of his hand. "I guessed it! The boy is a poet."

I shot a defiant look at him but he remained insultingly cool. The pretty girl interposed kindly, "Your feelings for the guitar may be a little exaggerated," she said, "but your enthusiasm certainly makes it just that more attractive. Are you going to Madrid?"

"Yes, and I believe I'm going to give a concert at the *Ateneo*. May I have your name so I can ask your parents' permission to invite you to it?"

"My name is Maria Querol."

At that moment I felt I would be saying that name very often in later life.

It was quite a burden for my young shoulders: to open up a new road for the guitar, beginning by trying to change the low opinion of it shared by the vast majority of my countrymen. True, Tárrega had been the apostle of the beloved instrument during his whole life, but the scope of his noble work did not equal the intensity of his devotion. He performed mostly in private rather than in public, more often before guitar aficionados with little musical education than before true experts or professional musicians. Consequently, he could not achieve significant changes in the general feeling about the artistic value of our neglected instrument.

Moreover, as a teacher, Tárrega had a following mainly made up of mediocre students—with the exception, of course, of Miguel Llobet, who had a solid background, excellent technique, and good judgment. He was a resourceful harmonist and also a fine transcriber.

The fact remains that, in the Spain of that time, the guitar was generally believed to be good only to accompany popular songs and folk tunes—or, as the wild boar on the train put it, to make music at parties featuring wine, women, and song. This amusing encounter at the grass-roots level can illustrate how strong was the feeling which prevailed then regarding the guitar:

One day, when I arrived at the Hotel Alameda in Granada, I began practicing early, keeping the sound as low as possible so as not to disturb the guests in the rooms adjoining mine. I had asked for my breakfast to be sent up. When the maid came in with the tray and saw me with guitar in hand, she winked and said, with an impish smile, "So early and already so gay, sir?"

6

In MADRID I took a room on Príncipe Street at a modest pension which a Sevillian friend had recommended. The owner, Don Gumersindo, walked the halls of his domains with a monkey sitting on his shoulder. He ascribed miraculous powers to the pet. Rooms were rented only on the approval of the four legged host, whom his master called "Romanones," after the famous politician of that time. Don Gumersindo's blind faith in his monkey's special talents dated back to a year or so before my arrival, when a young Andalusian student had rented a room at the pension. Polite and good-looking, the young man was liked by the guests, the maids, and the owner himself. Only the monkey refused to be charmed; he would become furious whenever the Andalusian attempted to pet him. Several weeks passed, and one morning Don Pablito, as the rogue was called, was missing from the house. He had disappeared without paying back rent, taking a collection of clothes, jewels, and other objects from the rooms of guests and staff. So complete was his disappearance that the police were never able to trace him.

"Romanones was the only one who smelled the rat," a guest said to console the crestfallen Don Gumersindo.

"You have an excellent psychologist in your pet," another said.

"Monkeys are the animals which best understand man. After all, we descend from them," asserted a hunchbacked old man whose ugly looks gave added weight to his theory. "Your monkey, Don Gumersindo, is outstanding," the old man continued. "If I were you, I'd put that clairvoyance of his to good use. Let him help you keep an eye on your guests. Maybe you'll catch a worse crook than Don Pablito someday!"

These and other suggestions had their impact on Don Gumersindo's troubled mind and, taking them seriously, he began to test the various theories. The first step was to compare the monkey's reactions to his own, while he was interviewing prospective guests. The similarity of their reactions was extraordinary! Within a very short time, he found he could not disagree with Romanones. Finally, he relied entirely on the monkey's judgment. When strangers came to ask for a room, Don Gumersindo would feign absentmindedness and not give them an answer until he had seen how his oracle reacted. If Romanones jabbered shrilly and made aggressive moves, then the prognosis was bad; when he grimaced happily and jumped about, the outlook for the guest was excellent. This amusing comedy attracted not only the guests of the house, but also outsiders, and Don Gumersindo became the butt of many a joke in the neighborhood.

I was assigned a large, cheerful, and not badly furnished room, with its own balcony overlooking the street, so the general opinion was that I had been received with special warmth by the pet. The master, however, without openly contradicting Romanones, took steps to protect himself from any simian error by asking for his money in advance.

Meetings between Romanones and me were both frequent and affectionate. Whenever I left the house, he would lie in wait for me, always ready to greet me on my return, demanding his due in the form of small pieces of fruit I had set aside from the none-too-generous helpings at the table, or searching my pockets for little tidbits I would bring in for him.

Very early one morning, I heard him at my door. I let him in. He jumped on me, trailing the other end of the chain, which usually was in his master's hand. He began searching my pockets with expert ease and when he found them empty, I had to pet him in compensation. Soon he was curled up in my arms, making the guttural sounds with which he usually indicated contentment. Carefully, I placed him on a chair, took the added precaution of tying his chain to the arm, and went back to my daily exercise on the guitar. The first chords terrified him; he began to scream and cry as if he were being beaten, but soon he calmed down and became extremely curious. Pulling at his chain, he tried to come closer to investigate the source of the sounds. I kept on working and noticed that little by little, he was being overcome by the subtle opiate of the music. Now he was perfectly quiet, his sad little eyes following the movements of my hands. The comic twitching of his body stopped, as if the very vitality of his being were now concentrated in the effort to listen and understand.

About an hour later, I heard heavy footsteps in the hall. The door opened to reveal the eccentric figure of Don Gumersindo, a look of anguish in his eye. It was the time of day the express trains from Andalusia and Catalonia would be arriving in Madrid, and with them some prospective boarders. Don Gumersindo was looking for his assistant. He heaved a sigh of relief when he saw us together.

"I was afraid he had escaped."

"No, he came to listen to me," I said, smiling. "Why not let him stay and give him a holiday?"

Observing that his master was closing in on him to take him away, Romanones began to shout frantically, as if denying accommodations to some unwelcome traveler. Annoyed, Don Gumersindo struck him, and the monkey replied in kind by biting his hand. There were shouts, threats, imprecations, angry commands from the master and angrier cries from the monkey who, having escaped from the man's hands, now jumped all

47

over the furniture, finally coming to rest on my shoulder, apparently seeking refuge. Attracted by the noise, maids and neighbors rushed in and stayed on to laugh. My room had been transformed into a circus, full of merriment and confusion. The monkey finally made his escape through the door and down the stairs. In hot pursuit, Don Gumersindo took the time to stop and hurl at me: "You've driven my poor monkey mad with your guitar! Pack your bags and get out!"

"He's jealous," said the chambermaid who took care of my room. "He's jealous because it's not a *he* monkey but a *she!*" Modestly lowering her voice to a whisper, she added, "I know. I looked the other day."

7

ONE OF THE FIRST THINGS I did in Madrid was go to the workshop of Manuel Ramírez, a famous guitar maker who had recently been granted the high-sounding title of "Luthier" by the Royal Conservatory of Madrid. It was a justly deserved honor to a good craftsman who always sought to perfect his skills—unlike others in his trade who more often than not seemed satisfied to turn out mediocre instruments.

I was still using the guitar I had acquired years before at Benito Ferrer's in Granada, thanks to my friend Miguel Cerón. It was really only good for practicing, and I dreamed of having another, more powerful and resonant instrument to go with the plans I had made for my artistic career.

At that time I was tall and skinny with long black hair flowing under a wide-brimmed hat, tortoise-shell glasses, a wide, full cravat like the ones some provincial photographers wore to give themselves artistic airs, a black velvet jacket fastened up to my neck with silver buttons, a long gray double-breasted overcoat, striped pants, patent-leather shoes and, in my hand, a sturdy cane to further enhance my image. I was barely eighteen years old.

As I entered his shop, Ramírez took one look at me and almost burst out laughing. He didn't go quite that far; instead, he launched into the most unsettling display of subtle mockery.

"And what may I do for the gentleman?" he asked me, with exaggerated obeisance. "It shall be a pleasure to wait on you."

Utterly disconcerted, I managed to look him right in the eye.

"My name is Andrés Segovia. I am a guitarist, and mutual friends in Córdoba suggested I see you."

His expression changed, but he did not drop his smile. He held out his hand to me.

"Yes, your name has reached this house. It seems that all of Seville flocked to the hall to hear you last year."

His words reminded me of *this* year's scant crowds and I turned as red as a tomato. Suspecting Ramírez was exaggerating his praise for some purpose of his own, I pretended I didn't hear him and continued, "I arrived in Madrid a few days ago and am planning to give a concert at the *Ateneo*. Mr. Ramírez, the guitar I have at present cannot live up to what I ask it to do, I need the best instrument you have available. Of course, I think it only reasonable that you set a moderate fee for this type of arrangement, like the one music stores make when they rent out a piano for a concert. If necessary, I am prepared to pay in advance."

Ramírez had been listening to me carefully and probably had even forgotten my appearance; his look was different, but he finally did burst out laughing.

"By God, that's not a bad offer! It's the first time it's been made to me but it does make sense. If Erard and Pleyel pianos are rented out for concerts, why not a Ramírez guitar?"

Opening the inner door to his workshop he motioned me to follow him.

50

His best workers were in the shop headed by the expert Santos Hernández. Ramírez asked him to bring one of his best guitars. He handed it to me and I looked it over slowly before trying it out for sound. The beauty of its curves, the old gold hues of the veins in the wood of the face, the delicate inlaid ornamentation edging the perfect rosette, the slender neck of lignum-vitae rising from the simple lines of the bosom to end in a small, elegant head . . . the graceful lines and the splendor of its body possessed my heart as swiftly as would the features of a heaven-sent woman suddenly appearing to become the loving companion of a lifetime.

I cannot describe the joy I felt as I began to finger it. The sound of the basses was both deep and mellow, those of the trebles, limpid and vibrating. Forgetting everything that surrounded me, I played it for a long time, going over all I had learned to play until then. Such was my delight that I tried to divide myself into two persons, one feeling the actual joy of making music on such a wonderful instrument, the other listening with delight as if, in the distance, someone else were actually playing it.

I knew then that this guitar was the tool with which I was to fulfill my musical destiny; at its mere touch I felt my commitment revitalized. I raised my head to beg Ramírez to let me have it at once but stopped short when I saw an old but sprightly handsome gentlemen who looked like the romantic musicians of an earlier age. Apparently he had slipped into the shop while I was playing and had been listening quietly.

"Bravo, young fellow, bravo! I like your temperament and your technique," he said. "What a pity such skill should be wasted on the small and undeveloped world of the guitar. Beautiful, perhaps, but solitary and wild; few men of talent have ventured there and you have chosen to spend on it all *your* God-given talent—why not consider changing instruments? You are still young enough; you could become famous playing the violin." Coming toward me with a cordial but grave look, he added, "I will give you all the help I can."

With a voice ringing like a churchbell, Ramírez explained solemnly, "Young man, *this* is Don José del Hierro, head professor of advanced violin studies at the Royal Conservatory."

I stood up to greet him respectfully.

"Thank you, maestro," I said, controlling my emotion. "I am afraid it is too late for me to take up another instrument but, in any case, I would never turn my back on the guitar. It needs me; the violin doesn't. Compare the history of the two instruments and you will know what I mean. If centuries ago musicians of moderate talent and less luck, like Nerula or Fortuna, had not devoted their love and work to the violin, it would not be the prince of all bowed instruments today. I shall be happy to accomplish their humble task for the guitar of tomorrow." And I added, "I have also sworn to walk in the steps of the sainted Francisco Tárrega, who lived and died for his beloved instrument, with little hope of glory or gain."

"Did you ever meet him?" Don José asked.

"No, but he is as known to me as if I had spent years at his side. He created the soul of the guitar."

"You are going to have a tough time, young fellow, but you've made your own choice. I hope you don't lose heart."

I glanced at Ramírez to let him know how much I wanted to take possession of "my" guitar. He guessed what I had in mind. Seized by a feeling of selflessness and generosity, he said, "Take it, kid. It's yours. Make it flourish in your hands with your good work. And, don't worry about the cost. Pay me back with something other than money. You understand?"

I embraced him, fighting back tears of gratitude.

"This is an invaluable gesture that has no price, Señor Ramírez," I said, but my voice was so low and broken that my words were hardly audible even to myself.

8

For more than a week I found it impossible to sleep; the joy of owning that guitar kept me awake. If finally exhausted I did doze off, I would soon reproach myself for my neglect, and my ingratitude alone would wake me up. Sleepless and nervous, I tossed and turned and would end up getting out of bed to look at the guitar, enthralled, not as one would look at an inanimate object but as someone who leans over to admire an active, dynamic, living thing. Only fear of disturbing my neighbors so late at night held me back from taking it out of its velvet-lined case and playing it softly, in a kind of lyrical caress.

While the date of my concert at the *Ateneo* was being set —something which was not without its difficulties—my pocketbook was becoming alarmingly slim. I was tortured by the thought that my money would run out in "*la Villa y*

Entrance to the Prado Museum.
Drawing by Bobri, Madrid 1971.

Corte," as the Spanish capital was called at one time. Thriftily, I stretched the little that remained.

Pepe Chacón, my friend from Córdoba who was then studying in Madrid, took it upon himself to show me the most beautiful and interesting city sights. He was friendly, sharp and intelligent. Being short annoyed him terribly, and he would raise his nasal voice as if that would add some height to his stature. The unfavorable opinion he had of his own appearance frequently made him harsh and transformed his usually timid words into wounding verbal explosions.

"What do you expect?" he would ask, pointing to himself up and down, half cynically, half dramatically. "If I didn't talk nonsense, nobody would notice me."

I was his frequent guest at concerts, theaters, lectures. It was he who first took me to the Prado Museum. How dazzling it was to pass from the grimness of our everyday world into that universe full of the marvelous dreams and strange visions of the artist seeking to play the role of God! Music had often protected me from harsh reality by transporting me into spaces without form, without words, without light, where enjoyment was only the flowing purity of sound, where I craved nothing but the timeless extension of the joy I felt. Until I entered the Prado, I had never penetrated that magic circle where immortal, fantastic lives had been enshrined against a background which the perceptive vision of the painter had transformed into a world more perfect than reality.

At first I gulped it all in at random, but soon I was stopping to relish my pleasures. Through the frames I could enter another world, another existence, and take possession of their landscapes and their scenes. Velázquez's great power attracted me most; he made me step over the threshold of his art. This is no mere exaggeration; Théophile Gautier, overcome by *Las Meninas*, once asked, "Where is the painting?"

Purposely ignoring other schools and painters, I concentrated on El Greco and Goya, so different and yet so complementary, who had put on canvas such masterful visions of the Spanish soul. What lucid renderings of Spanish life and history! Everything which is to be admired in our people, everything heroic and indomitable—and, alas, so often the reverse, too—is in their works, living entities from which neither good nor bad can be subtracted without destroying their very existence. Because of my youth and lack of experience in that field I could not appreciate the technical aspects of the paintings I was seeing. But my sensitivity to visual art was being awakened by a natural affinity, just as it had in music. It wasn't difficult to perceive the beauty of certain forms and the play of lights surrounding them. Ahead of understanding, I was almost guessing the superlative values that went beyond the aesthetic and psychological blend I found in those works of art.

I must have been deep in such thought, for Pepe Chacón said softly, "Hey, you're very quiet."

"I'm trying to see all that went into these paintings, but I don't have the training," I think I said. "I keep asking them questions, but I get no answers . . . or they speak back in a language of which I know only a few words. Still, it is a consolation to know that I am moved by the whole, that my reaction is legitimate: I am in complete accord with what I see."

"You're on the right track, then. Intuition will get you there ahead of reason. Let me give you a little example of what I mean. I like to come to the Prado on Sunday mornings. Admission is free then, and it's fun to hear what common people say about these works. Often it's a mixutre of nonsense and perception; it can be very revealing. For instance, the other Sunday I followed a young couple to this room—humble working-class people. We were looking at the El Grecos. The husband fell behind, but the girl went straight to stand in front of the *Gentleman with His Hand on His Breast*. She looked at it for a long time. Then she turned to her husband and called him over. 'Look, darling, look,' she exclaimed, smiling, excited. 'Doesn't he seem real?' She spoke with such affection, I swear she could have been talking about the portrait of a relative she had suddenly discovered here."

I laughed. Pepe went on. "I'll bet El Greco must have looked down from his Olympian niche and felt more flattered by that simple girl's discovery than he had been by all the erudite opinions of the art critics who praise his work. Can't

you see, her instinct told her that the austere man in the painting had been endowed with such a powerful transfusion of
life by the painter that, without losing his own personality,
he had become the very symbol of Spanish man."

9

I WANTED TO MEET Daniel Fortea, one of Tárrega's last pupils, and finally got my wish one day when I went to Ramírez's workshop. Fortea was just leaving as I came in the door and Ramírez stopped him to introduce us. As it was the first time I had had the good fortune to meet a guitarist who had studied under the late master, the encounter was very imporant to me.

He was about twenty-five, of medium build; his slightly elongated face and prominent cheekbones lent him a hard, unfriendly look, tempered somewhat by an easy and spontaneous laugh. His narrow forehead was capped by long hair, carefully and artificially waved, coming down to his collar, his eyes had the impish glint of a rascal. He was correctly but modestly dressed. His general attitude seemed to claim unconditional admiration.

He granted me the honor of shaking my hand. His was surprisingly gnarled and rough. How I envied him the memory of Tárrega and the echo of the master's sweet plaything which, undoubtedly, was still alive in his soul! Expectantly I waited, hoping to hear enthralling details of their friendship or, should he condescend to play for me, to reveal his share of the heritage Tárrega had left his pupil.

Such was not my luck. The cheerful Fortea limited himself to telling off-color jokes. True, at my open and friendly challenge he took up a guitar but only to play some mediocre composition of his own. How disillusioned I was! Obviously Fortea had received little of the master's mantle; the influence had been minimal. Had he rebelled against it? What were Tárrega's other students like?

Fortea gave no signs of wanting to hear me play although Ramírez had praised me to the skies. "Ramírez tells me you are giving a concert at the *Ateneo*. Perhaps I should give you some advice about your program, interpretation, tone, et cetera. You can call at my house in the afternoons between four and five."

I declined his offer but went on to suggest timidly that he might allow me to copy some of Tárrega's unpublished transcriptions, a treasure he and other faithful custodians preserved. He laughed sarcastically at my suggestion.

"Oh, that would be most difficult to arrange," he said. "They're in Valencia."

His laugh mortified me more than his refusal. Not wishing to appear put out, I answered his laugh with one of my own. If his had meant I was not worthy of being entrusted with such treasures, mine conveyed the belief he would neither give nor lend them out because he was afraid someone else might play them better than he could himself.

Taking my leave of Ramírez, I was more convinced than ever that I had to free the guitar from such jailers by creating a repertoire, open to all, which would end once and for all the exclusivity of those "inherited jewels." I thought of going to Joaquín Turina and Manuel de Falla—they were already known—and to other famous composers . . . I would act as their guide through the labyrinth of the guitar's technique. I would see to it that their musical ideas came to life in the instrument. I convinced myself, at that moment, that they would become firm believers in the guitar.

It did not take me long to see the reverse of the coin. My resolve was shaken. How pretentious I was! Did I really think any of these great men would follow the bidding of a mere beginning artist? I listened to the common sense preached by this small internal voice and went back to my modest daily tasks.

"Señorito, you're being eaten up by that damned guitar! I'd die of jealousy if you were my boyfriend," was how the cheerful maid who cleaned by room put it.

Indeed, I was getting very thin. I spent my days trying out new transcriptions, devising ever more complex exercises, going over and over again the pieces I had chosen for my concert. The stingy host of the boardinghouse also shared some of the blame; the meals he provided for his guests were miserly. My singleness of purpose and the poor food were undermining my otherwise good health. Little fresh air and even less sun did the rest.

I had been feeling feverish in the late afternoons and generally overcome by a new lassitude. On reaching the boardinghouse after my meeting with Fortea, this sensation had developed into severe pulsating pains in my temples. My eyes smarted as if sand had blown into them.

The unaccustomed silence from my room soon brought the maid.

"What's wrong, *señorito?*" she asked, at the door. "Why aren't you playing? Has your guitar caught a cold?"

Seeing me stretched out on the bed she came over and put her strong hand on my forehead.

"You've got a high fever! Do you have any relatives in Madrid?" I managed to shake my head. "You poor man, I'm going to get you something," and with this she put her sturdy self into action, ran from the room, and down the stairs.

I fell into an uncontrollable drowsiness. Some time must have passed before the girl's voice brought me back to reality; I struggled to raise my heavy eyelids. She was standing at the foot of the bed, blowing with all her strength on the contents of a cup she was holding. I smiled to myself and thought that the only contagious thing I could catch from her was good health! She put her arm under my pillow so that I could raise my head and swallow the awful mixture, sip by sip. She kept chattering away, the metallic tone of her voice beating in my ears.

"The boss went out with his wife. She's a strange duck but he is a demon! No one cares for them—that's God's justice, isn't it? But we're all very fond of you even if we laugh at you a little. What can you expect, though, with that long hair and that funny tie of yours. You're very kind . . . and we love to hear you play the guitar, you really make it talk. If only you played some *malagueñas* instead of all that classy stuff! If I were your sweetheart I'd stop you from hugging that guitar; strumming, strumming, strumming, all the time! No pasttimes, no girls, no fun." She stopped to feel my pulse, then continued, anxiety creeping into her voice. "*Señorito*, you're getting worse. I'm going to call the cook; we'll get your clothes off and you into bed."

That was the last I heard. Slipping off into the worst delirium of my life, I spent three days in a coma, as I was told later. My fantasy wandered at will and I was beset by hallucinations, nightmares and extreme anxiety. One dream, which tormented me most, escaped from the subconscious to remain forever in my mind. I can't resist the temptation to recall it. . . .

A swarm of lizards, large ugly birds, cats, and monkeys, were attacking me as I lay in bed. I was fending them off as best I could, kicking at them and beating them back with my hands. But there was no letup. Some of the animals were pecking at my head, others scratched my hands, some made horrible grimaces at me and moaned like wailing violins; the noise was infernal. They stopped, suddenly, waiting expectantly, and this paralyzed me. I could not lift a finger. Something terrible was about to happen!

Climbing over the mound formed by my feet under the bedclothes came a little mouse. Slowly it inched forward, its bright, mocking little eyes fixed on mine. My fear became indescribable. When the mouse had reached my chin, it leaped suddenly, put its small paws on my upper lip and dug its sharp teeth into my nose. I felt no pain, strangely enough, only fright as I saw that my nose, as the mouse pulled away, was stretching, stretching. Slowly the mouse backed away to the end of the bed and suddenly let go of its prize. My nose snapped back like a rubber band, giving me a painful slap and I cried out. At this the other animals cheered the mouse, their laughs comically orchestrated in different keys, and the scene was repeated two or three times.

Years later, a painter used my dream as a subject for a series of amusing drawings; a disciple of Freud wrote a profound treatise about it in which, needless to say, I did not appear in a very good light.

When the fever subsided and I regained consciousness, my first surprise was to find totally unknown faces about me, some sullen, others expressing concern.

"So, we're feeling better, eh?" asked a coarse-looking man. In his toothless smile, ill-shaven chin, and crossed eyes I thought I recognized one of the beasts in my dream.

"You gave us a lot of trouble, trying to keep you in bed," another added, this one looking very much like one of the birds which had pecked at me.

"Thank God that's over!" exclaimed a very, very old woman, one of those wrinkled old women one sees only in Castile; Théophile Gautier claimed that the province is called Old Castile because only there does one find such faces.

I soon learned that it was my humanitarian maid who had rallied the servants and guests against the owner—he wanted to ship me off to a hospital the moment he knew I was ill. A medical student who had the room next to mine got one of his professors to come and the diagnosis reassured the innkeeper: my case was not contagious; I had a very high fever probably caused by nervous exhaustion. Adding to her heavy work burden, the maid took on the task of caring for me—but only, as she told me later, up to a point; for *certain* tasks she counted on the cook, a man, or on the waiters in the dining room. Even her mother had been enlisted to stand by and watch over me when household duties or sleep overcame her or her assistants.

After searching the corners of my room eagerly, with increasingly frightened eyes, I finally let out a yell: "WHERE IS MY GUITAR!!!"

"The boss took it," the cross-eyed man replied. "I don't know if to sell or pawn it, just in case you owed him some rent."

"Bandit! Son-of-a-bitch!" I exploded, jumping out of bed only to fall flat on my face, my knees buckling under me.

Mariana, the maid, rushed into the room, alarmed at my scream and the ensuing commotion. "Oh, I'm late! I knew you'd miss it, so I went to the boss's room and took it back. Here it is!"

"What a kid!" said the man who looked like one of my birds; his voice was both bitter and wistful. "She can be kind and considerate as a duchess. Except with me."

To me, Mariana's heart was as sweet as a little pear in honey, as we say down south in my country.

Daniel Fortea

10

A FEW DAYS LATER, Pepe Chacón burst into my room with this news:

"Let me say first that we've already set the date for your concert at the *Ateneo*, but it wasn't easy. The younger ones who head the music section were dead set against it and turned down my request for the hall. Then I appealed to the fat cats who run the *Ateneo*. *They* were shocked at the thought that I, a mere student, would dare approach them with such a wild idea. They've appointed themselves the keepers of the *Ateneo*'s chastity, and they sleep like Argus, with fifty eyes open. I tell you, I didn't know where to turn. Their Eminences were crossing themselves at the thought of a sacrilegious spree in the hall, while the young ones snickered at the word "music," when I mentioned that your repertoire includes Haydn, Mozart, Schubert . . . They actually believed I was talking about some hilarious musical parody! Even my best friends there, who pretended to be on my side, proposed that we let it go for next year, when the schedule of activities is expected to be less crowded—you know, hoping the whole thing would be shelved or forgotten by then. All they really wanted was to avoid a musical scandal of *lèse culture!*

"But wait. I was about to give up, when along came José María Izquierdo. He has an open mind and he heard you play in Seville. Well, he joined forces with me, he shared the explaining and, above all, the persisting. And, since he enjoys a very solid reputation at the *Ateneo*, it was smooth sailing from then on."

"I've never met him," I said, "but they speak very highly of him in Seville. They say he's very knowledgeable and has suprisingly original ideas. I'm glad the guitar has gained such a champion!"

"Now it is up to you," Pepe continued. "You have to pierce the deaf ears of those people and straighten their twisted conception of the guitar. Your concert has to justify what they consider our audacity. They must be put in a position of having to congratulate us! Choose the best of your repertoire and play like an angel!"

Beaming with happiness, I told him, "You know more than the devil about what goes on in Heaven, so if you assure me that angels play the guitar then I can die happy," and, I added facetiously, "I'd hate to go to sleep someday in this world, with a guitar in my hands, and wake up in the next playing a harp. They haven't made much musical progress there; they still stick to harp and organ."

My night of trial, like that of a knight errant, was so near, and the event so decisive for my career, that I turned to studying more intensely than ever and cut off all ties with the outside world. I lived in seclusion in my room, forgetting time and doing without all but the most indispensable activities. Many nights I slept very little, muting the strings with cloth and forging ahead tirelessly, cleaning up difficult passages of even the most imperceptible flaws.

Only Mariana would come now and then to break into my solitude, bringing with her that picaresque chatter of popu-

Portrait of Andrés Segovia by Palmer, Madrid 1917.

lar Madrid. Or very late, she would steal into my room and, seeing me still at work, would pretend to get angry and scold me. Taking the guitar from me she would put it in its case and then gently push me toward the bed. Finally, when my eyes had closed, she would quietly slip away.

One night the landlady surprised her in my room. Mariana was terrified. The landlady had taken advantage of her husband's animallike sleep and, as usual, was heading for the nearby room of a heroic and ever-alert artillery officer. The girl tried to leave my room, but the landlady, believing she might profit somehow by the incident, barred the door. Giving her extended arm the vigor which, due to the late hour, she could not lend her voice, she said, "Get out!"

"Oh, please, *señora*, don't fire me! I'm a decent girl. I promise to work for two at no extra pay! Don't fire me!" Mariana's appeal seemed to come from her very soul.

To get double the work out of a maid without having to pay more appeared to be something the landlady would consider. Softening the accusing tone of her voice and relaxing the angry sweep of her arm, she changed her warning: "Go to your room, girl. Quickly!"

Mariana fled.

The landlady turned to me and tapped her foot on the tiled floor rhythmically with a meaningful "You sly fox, you!"

11

THE CONCERT AT THE *Ateneo* was discouraging for a boy as inexperienced and fainthearted as I was. Because it showed no immediate result, it seemed to be a disaster which would be difficult for me to overcome, and that thought secretly shamed me. My savings were dwindling at a frightening rate, too; I had only enough funds to tide me over another week, with no prospects beyond that. Worse yet, I would have died rather than reveal my impecunious situation even to my closest friend.

Ramírez sent me a message to come to see him, and I went reluctantly. My pessimism painted everything black; I thought the good luthier was as disappointed as I by my concert and was looking for some nice way to regain possession of the guitar he had so spontaneously let me take on credit.

"Ah, here is the artist at last!" was his welcome. I thought his smile was sarcastic.

"I'm still not too well," I answered, avoiding his eyes. "The fever comes back now and then, I'm getting over it very slowly."

"No one would have thought you lacked plenty of strength the other night. What power! What passion! I was deeply moved to hear how four small pieces of wood I had together could produce such beautiful music. I've never been so proud of my work. When I heard the audience applaud you so enthusiastically, I wanted to stand up and say, 'Hey, throw a few handclaps my way! I have a right to share a little in this triumph; if it weren't for me, it could have taken you a lot longer to meet this artist or to fully appreciate his music.' You know, the morning after the concert I congratulated my technicians, particularly this quiet one, my best," he said, pointing to Santos Hernández.

His words were like balm to me, but I still poured my heart out to him.

"I'm upset at the negative results, Señor Ramírez. It's true that the audience applauded, that friends and even strangers came up to congratulate me, but other things were more important to me than flattery. Some of Madrid's famous musicians were there, and not one of them came up to speak to me afterwards, not even to say something about the guitar. Their silence alone showed contempt and proved the futility of my effort. I felt nothing but shame and defeat.

"And the press didn't bother to print a single word about the event, either. I've been scouring the papers for the last ten days, and I haven't seen one mention of my name yet. It would be foolish of me to believe that the concert or the artist made a dent in town. Then, too, the great impresario I was expecting didn't show up, after all. So there went my dreams of contracts, travel, fame, wealth. The whole thing caved in on me like a sand castle. Now I don't know what to do, where to turn . . ."

"Jesus, you could drown in a thimble!" Ramírez exclaimed. "Chin up and listen to me. The musicians you speak of were surprised and favorably impressed; I heard them talk about it. They only regret you've taken up the guitar. You know, the same old thing. And if they didn't rush over to congratulate you, it's because you're still a babe and they are venerable, prominent figures and want to keep their distance—that's all. As for reviewers, our newspapers have none. The one who covers the bullfight is ipso facto the music critic—even if he knows less about it than my grandmother. Forget the impresario, we'll find another one. There are no concert specialists in Madrid, but even the dumbest can do it—once he smells a profit. Cheer up and stop worrying!"

He paused to let all that sink in. "Aren't you going to ask me why I sent for you? I almost feel like not telling you, but . . . here it is anyway. The director of a foreign bank in Madrid—a rare one because he's a music fan—wants you to play in his home. He offers two hundred *pesetas*. Do you accept?

"Accept?" I was wild with joy.

In time, I began hearing that my concert at the *Ateneo* had indeed been written about—in private letters. Friends and fate made it possible for me to read—even to own—some of those letters. They expressed opinions as diverse as their authors—men, women, musicians, dilettanti, random members of the audience who had heard me play that night. Witness, for instance, some fragments I am still able to reconstruct:

From Maria Querol, the pianist—none other than the young lady I had met on the train from Córdoba to Madrid—to her aunt:

. . . and the young man we met on the train finally gave his guitar concert at the Ateneo. I went with Cousin Paco . . . He looked pale and thinner to me. He did not include very important selections in his program, but strangely enough, I did not miss them. Even light fare seems to be ennobled by the guitar . . . . I was very moved. He played an exquisite Mendelssohn barcarolle which I myself have been playing ever since, although its delicate poetry is overwhelmed by the piano. Still, I play it, if only to recapture the thrill it gave me when I heard it that night on the guitar. . . . He received considerable applause, and it was both funny and sad to see how awkwardly he acknowledged it. Also, he wore a dinner jacket which was far too big for him, a loan, no doubt, from someone a lot heavier than himself . . .

At the end, I dragged Paco over so we both could congratulate him. Paco was reluctant—you know how Wagnerian he is—that intimate guitar music seemed too slight to him compared to the orchestral majesty of his idol. I wanted to thank the young man for sending us invitations and say a few kind words to him. After all, it was the least I could do. He was surrounded by friends, but he ran to me the moment he saw me. "How kind of you to come! I couldn't see you in the darkness, but I felt your presence in the hall," he told me. At that, Paco frowned and for a moment I didn't know what to say. Finally, embarrassed by the silence, I foolishly called attention to his ill-fitting dinner jacket, by saying, "You look very elegant." He turned red and became very serious, deeply wounded by the joke. "I see that my borrowed suit hasn't escaped your attention, *señorita*," he replied with bitter reproach.

His unexpected remark made me feel ashamed of my *faux pas* and, trying to repair the damage, I invited him to come to our house some afternoon. Paco didn't second the invitation, which annoyed me very much, but the young artist accepted immediately and his expression changed as if we had secretly made peace. He squeezed my hand as we said good-bye and barely nodded to Paco in farewell. "He's very self-confident," that silly Paco said as we left. . . . But that was a week ago, and we still haven't seen the young guitarist in our house. Will he come . . .?

And this, from another letter, one written by a typically supercilious member of the *Ateneo:*

I have little to say about that guitar concert because I didn't have the patience to sit it out so I left before the second part was over. That stupid young fellow is making useless efforts to change the guitar—with its mysterious, Dionysiac nature—into an Apollonian instrument. The guitar responds to the passionate exaltation of Andalusian folklore, but not to the precision, order, and structure of classical music. Only a fool would dare violate the laws which separate those two worlds; the flesh and the spirit, the senses and the intellect. The gods should punish him for his arrogance as they once punished Marsyas, though perhaps he doesn't deserve such a glorious end, only silence and oblivion.

The next one, by the most unlikely relays, fell into the hands of Ramírez, the guitar maker, and a few weeks later, into mine. It was written by a pupil of Tárrega whom I later nicknamed "the Tárregophore," because he seemed to carry the master around with him: he imitated his walk, his accent, his every gesture, as if to validate Benavente's amusing remark: "Blessed be our disciples, for theirs shall be the legacy of our faults." Of course, in the case of Tárrega, they were not faults but brilliant qualities which nonetheless became a caricature of the original when he was imitated by his pupils. The letter was sent to a Father Corell of Valencia:

. . . and despite the many blessings I received from you when I left for Madrid, I have nothing positive to report, dear Father. This town is like a stone wall when it comes to accepting artists from the provinces. What our beloved Tárrega must have suffered at the indifference of these enemies of the guitar! No wonder he left Madrid the moment he finished his early studies in the Royal Conservatory and went to teach instead in Valencia and Catalonia, where he made real friends and admirers of his art and personality, such as your humble servant. . . .

Let me give you an example of how misguided the people of Madrid are regarding the guitar. A few nights ago a young Andalusian guitarist gave a concert at the Ateneo. No one knows his real name—he must have called himself "Segovia" to get people's attention. He played a tasteless program; side by side with the master's transcriptions—in which he took unforgivable liberties—he dared play some of his own. His ease and self-confidence impressed the audience. After some initial reservations, they thought it best to grant him their applause. It was not a spontaneous success and barely a legitimate one. Why has this young man taken up the guitar? He is so far from understanding the blessed school of our beloved Tárrega! At first glance one can see that the position of his hands is very careless; if he does achieve speed and clarity in difficult passages it is due to a sort of fallible intuition, not because he applies the proper rules. Worst of all, dear Father: he plucks the strings with his fingernails!

. . . How was it possible for this self-taught artist to give a concert in the *Ateneo*? A mystery! They say he came from Seville well provided with letters of recommendation to the big shots in the capital. Maybe his true ability lies in playing Andalusian folk tunes and so he was able to fool the aficionados! . . . Meanwhile, here I am without influential sponsors. My fingers are getting rusty. And the possibility of my being accepted for a concert at the Fine Arts Circle is still very remote. . . .

Finally, let me quote a few lines from a letter written to Joaquín Turina by a composer friend:

When you spoke so highly of the guitar, of that Llobet or Llovet you said you heard in Paris, I thought it was another instance of your usual Andalusian exaggeration; but I have just heard a young guitarist at the *Ateneo*, and I am impressed by the wealth of possibilities offered by our popular instrument. The artist was a young man from Granada called Segovia, and known in Seville. He handles the strings with taste and dexterity. He played some fine little pieces by Tárrega and mostly transcriptions of minor classic and romantic works. I think the nature of the instrument is more suitable for the minor works of Albéniz and Malats, for instance. They tell me this young fellow even plays some Bach fugues. To me, this seems like teaching a dog to do clever tricks. What would really be interesting—if we knew the instrument better and if the guitar were to attract enough virtuosos—would be to create a typical Spanish repertoire for it. One as removed from the music played in the cafés as your Scola Cantorum (if you'll forgive the example).

I think these excerpts speak for the variety of impressions created by my concert, a lot better than I could, were I to try to narrate them.

12

ONE NIGHT my charming and tireless guide, Pepe Chacón, took me to the famous *Café de Levante* where writers, painters, musicians and other artists congregated. Some were older and celebrated, others young and still unknown; all however, were colorful, witty and spiced their speech with plenty of ribaldry. They gathered in mutually hostile and separate groups.

My provincial eyes searched for, and joyfully recognized, faces which constantly appeared in the press. At one table, presided by the imperious literary figure, Valle Inclán, were painter Julio Romero de Torres and his brother, Enrique; writers Pérez de Ayala, Moya del Pino, and satellite newspaper and magazine writers who picked up the crumbs that fell from this feast of the intellect.

The triangular head of Jacinto Benavente was visible at another table, surrounded by wild admirers and an occasional willowy young man of delicate sweet looks and gestures. Don Jacinto was at the height of his renown as a playwright and his recent play, *La Malquerida (The Passion Flower)*, had definitely established his fame both in Spain and in Spanish-speaking America; cities vied for the honor of his visits, theaters for the first run of his new plays, newspapers for the right to reprint those sparkling columns which appeared on Mondays in *El Imperial*. Benavente's every saying was passed from mouth to mouth. The huge sloth who signed his articles "El Caballero Audaz" ("The Daring Knight") but whose true name was José Carretero Novillo, was the frequent victim of Don Jacinto's epigrammatic darts. "He's right to call himself a cart driver (Carretero), but he's past the age of a young bull (Novillo)," Don Jacinto once said.

As usual, "El Caballero Audaz" reacted. One afternoon they met entering the *Gato Negro* cafe, and the furious journalist stepped in front of the slightly built Don Jacinto. "I'll never let a son-of-a-bitch go in before me!" he shouted. "But I will," Don Jacinto countered, stepping aside.

Naturally, Benavente was himself the frequent target of enemies and detractors. I cannot remember if it was then or later that he brought out the play *A Lady* but I cannot forget that within hours after it was first staged, a local poet had all of Madrid laughing over these lines:

Don Jacinto Benavente	Don Jacinto Benavente
ha estrenado Una Señora	has premiered *A Lady*.
y es lo que dice la gente	People are saying
¡ya era hora!	"It's about time he did!"

Here and there in the café, young artists, all of them iconoclasts, mostly in shirtsleeves, with unkempt long hair, and a few with ditto consciences, attracted general attention with their loud voices and violent attacks on the works of better-known men. Until fame smiled on them and rescued them from obscurity, these prematurely embittered young people preyed on those who had achieved success; few were spared their vitriolic comments. Fortunately, I escaped falling in step with them, my contemporaries. Somehow, life hadn't been all that hard on me; perhaps that is why I was able to

75

pass from youth to maturity without feeling growing pains too much, looking on the success of friends and enemies alike, with satisfaction and inner peace.

The local bourgeoisie came to the café, too, and gaped at the immortals, the embattled politicians—mostly of left-wing persuasion—and personalities of the theatrical world. Without exception they would lower their voices and settle back to listen to Corvino or Balsa, the former a highly regarded violinist of the Madrid Symphony, the latter a moderately skilled pianist; both played serious music each evening in the café. There was rapt silence for them except when the famous writer Ramón del Valle Inclán was present; his insensitivity to musical sound, like that of most Spanish men of letters, was known to all. He felt a secret pleasure in bringing down on himself the furious glances and shouted requests for silence from the music lovers in the café; he would answer these with caustic wit and ended up the center of attraction. (Perhaps this was his purpose.) The musicians, needless to say, understandably felt they were being insulted by this magnificent, garrulous and nonsensical enemy of music.

13

ON A MOONLESS but warm night in May, Pepe Chacón suggested to the group of friends gathered in my room, the odd idea of transferring our meeting to an abandoned cemetery on Fuencarral street where I could continue to play for them. The plan was received enthusiastically: we were at the age when anything contrary to common sense was popular. Only Manolo de Ubeda disapproved but since he usually took the contrary view on any subject, we disregarded his arguments and set out on our escapade.

About ten of us marched out into the night. The party included a Dr. Berenguer who, though older than us, had been accepted into our circle for his picaresque, often hilarious tales about the court of the sultan of Morocco, whose private physician he was.

Two of my friends carried the black guitar case on their

shoulders, as if it were a coffin. The rest of the company followed behind like a funeral procession, sighing deeply whenever a passerby stopped to look, or tip his hat, as he murmured, "poor soul!" Some voiced the more characteristic Madrid expression heard at a child's funeral: "Angels to Heaven and chocolate to the living!"

Climbing the cemetery wall, we looked around for something to sit on. The darkness and silence scared even the bravest among us. As our eyes became accustomed to the dark, we saw flickering lights or will-o'-the-wisps in the distance. Suddenly, we were stricken by the thought that we had come to disturb the dead. For a long time, we sat berating ourselves and each other for having fallen for this absurd idea.

Someone took the guitar out of its case and handed it to me. Softly, as if in a dream, I played the *andante* from Beethoven's Sonata No. 4. The Sublime Deaf One had poured his deepest and most poetic feeling into that movement; complaint and hope, question and answer, an austere, harmonious prayer which doubtless can move Heaven's feeling for man's nostalgic soul. Its short initial phrases, interspersed with moments of quiet reflection, lead to a broad flowing song which is in striking contrast to the emotional intervals of the first theme. This mystery is repeated in rapid, melodic smiles in the high register.

We felt overcome by the beauty of the piece, by its pure sound made so spiritual by the guitar, by the eerie atmosphere of the surroundings. I found it miraculous that my fingers could knit together the intricate sounds without mistakes, despite my feelings and the darkness.

When I finished, I put the guitar away and wouldn't play any more. Nor did anyone ask me to, either; it was as if by tacit agreement we could not try to improve on the music I had just played, or on what we had felt as we listened to it.

Some time passed in silence. Then Goy de Silva whispered; "Look, look!" One of the small distant lights was growing in size, it was coming towards us! It stopped, still some distance away.

"Who goes there?" The voice was hoarse and insecure. Half-questioning, half-pleading, it repeated, "Who goes there?"

Our silence showed our fear, but Chacón managed to overcome his.

"It must be the caretaker." His voice was hesitant.

"We are people of peace," someone in the group called out, giving the time-honored signal of peaceful intentions.

Indeed, it was the caretaker who had heard soft, ethereal music and had been scared out of his wits. Discovering we were flesh and bone and, by our voices, young to boot, he gave us a tongue-lashing which did not spare our feelings. However, the thought that we might be drunk or ready for a fight, made him lower his tone. "If you don't leave immediately, I'll blow my whistle and call the police."

"Calm down, my good man," said Fernando Fortún. "You don't have to talk of profanation or drunkards. We are all students, artists, musicians, and we came . . ."

"Guard," broke in Dr. Berenguer, fearing a lyrical harangue by the poet might lead to worse, "take this *duro* and have a drink on us tomorrow. Now, please unlock the gate for us."

The tale does not end here, but to finish it I must skip ahead a few years. Goy de Silva published in *La Esfera*, a Madrid weekly, an account of that night's adventure and, among other things, proved his memory to be deliciously inexact. In his fantasy he added Tórtola Valencia dancing naked around the tombstones to a dreamy Chopin nocturne played by me. The article appeared a few days before the annual masked ball of the Barcelona Círculo Artístico, which I attended. There was Tórtola, the center of a group of artists and newspaper people.

"Andrés," she called out with her ever-present English accent, "Goy de Silva must have dreamed up that story!"

I looked her straight in the face, without batting an eye. "But Tórtola, could you possibly have forgotten such a night?"

She hesitated. "Of course, Andrés, how stupid of me! How could I have forgotten?"

Still more years passed. In 1923 I went to give my first concert in Mexico City. One of those difficult journalists came to see me at my hotel, asking for an interview.

"This morning Tórtola Valencia described in detail the

night she danced naked to your music, in a Madrid cemetery," he started out. "Can you tell me what you remember about the incident? It would be interesting to give both versions in my article."

"I can tell you about it, but only for your private information and if you promise not to use it," I answered.

He gave me his word that no mention would be made of it in his story which would be based on other subjects covered in the interview.

"I shall not mention Tórtola Valencia in my story!"

Reassured, I described in detail what had actually taken place, including Goy de Silva's flights of fancy and Tórtola's suddenly recovering her memory at the masked ball in Barcelona. We both laughed and, after asking a few routine questions, the man left. By the end of that very week he had published his story—which included everything he had promised not to use.

A few days later I met Tórtola again, this time in Mexico's Spanish Club. She rushed over to me.

"Andrés, could you possibly have forgotten such a night? Is it possible?" she said with significant emphasis, feigning such burning rage I thought my eyeglasses would melt.

"Of course, Tórtola, how stupid of me! It was so many years ago—how could I have forgotten?"

14

I WOULD LIKE TO PAUSE and introduce some of the friends and acquaintances who were part of my world during that first stay in Madrid. They were—or became—musicians, writers, artists, a few of them honored today in the Spanish-speaking world.

Some readers acquainted with Spanish culture may recognize the names prominent in the theater and literature. They are interwoven in my long and varied life, and I feel I should introduce them now.

We met frequently at the *Café de Levante*. The *tertulia*, as a gathering of intellectuals is called, was composed mostly of Pepe Chacón and his friends from the *Ateneo* who had made my concert possible. Varied as most human groups are, most of this *tertulia's* members were friendly, lively and witty. Some, it must be confessed, were pedantic, even arrogant.

Needless to say, I took to those whose ideas and feelings I shared, giving as wide a berth as possible to the others.

Of the latter, the most *pelmazo*—to use the Andalusian expression meaning a colossal bore—was Manolo de Ubeda. He was of medium height, and somewhat paunchy with a pale even bloodless, face. He affected extremely fine pince-nez and through the eggshell-thin lenses peered his intelligent, expressive, but domineering gaze. He was highly cultured and in time became known as a translator whose work, though accurate, was nevertheless too cold and dry for my taste. He achieved some fame in literary circles and in the 1930s, during the Republic, did a stint in the diplomatic service.

Because his family was wealthy, he had been able in his youth to build up an excellent library where he buried his budding ideas. He changed intellectual stars often, always embracing the last one so completely, that Manolo himself reached, as we claimed, a state of "Manololessness" which made him but the echo of the books he kept in his library. He read a lot but perceived little.

Manolo had the good fortune to become engaged, and later to marry, an extremely attractive blond and graceful young woman from Madrid, Maruja Montoro. Theirs was a case of selective affinity, for Maruja had flirted with such solemn gentlemen as Homer, Cicero, Goethe, Hegel and many others; she was proud that she could quote extensively from them all. I felt that if these men had been alive it might just be possible that none of them—no matter how wise—could have refused a brief but sweet respite from erudition with lovely Maruja.

Manolo was self-satisfied even about having her as his fiancée; it was rumored that once, when they found themselves alone, he took her tenderly in his arms and whispered into her ear, "I don't dare congratulate myself on being the most fortunate being on earth, but indeed, I can say that I am very close to one who could!"

Another of the daily companions was the always diligent and sharp Pepe Chacón. Less often, we saw Pedro Salinas, with his enlightened words and harsh voice, whose poetic fire, to me, was more like smoldering embers than a burning flame.

Another poet, also a playwright, was Francisco Villaespesa, many of whose sonnets I knew by heart at that time and can barely recall today. Villaespesa has not been given his full due in Spain, but it is a fact that the severest critics of a Spanish artist are those from his own country, particularly if they belong to his close circle of friends.

"He's really clever," someone at the *tertulia* would say.

"Who's that?" a doubting regular would ask.

"So-and-so."

"What do you mean, clever? He's a friend of mine!"

Lastly, there was José María Izquierdo, who was worth more than any of us. His premature death was a great loss to Spanish letters, and what he left is only a pale reflection of his true talent, though it does mirror his exquisite spirit. Extremely sensitive to the arts, Izquierdo could understand good music by instinct, if not by habit or knowledge. The fervor of his voice, which had neither emphatic highs nor lows, compelled us to adopt his opinions as if they were beliefs.

Occasionally, the group would be joined by a Señor Egónez, a rich, vain dilettante who had had a mechanical organ installed in his home; he spent rainy days pedaling out rolls of Schubert—his musical skills were not up to anything else. I also met Pepito Zamora there, a tragicomic error of nature. Neither he nor his sister could agree on their sexes. More feminine than effeminate, his stance, voice, gestures, and inclinations were those of a woman; his sister, on the other hand, had a jutting jaw, a deep voice, and the glare of an eagle when she looked at the other girls in her school. Pepito was clever at sketching; following his vocation and disregarding his family's pleas, he went into the world of fashion.

He was constantly shadowed by the Marquis de Hoyos y Vinent, a novelist of somewhat limited talents, of the same persuasion as Pepito. When they were at our *tertulia*, the pair kept us in stitches with their derisive wit. Once, Pepito told us, his sister had shouted at him: "You fairy!" to which he had countered, "Next to you, anybody is one!" Pepito's father had once taken him to task and, shaking him roughly by the shoulder, had berated him: "Boy, don't you understand that I want only strong he-men around?"

To which Pepito replied; "Yes, Daddy, and so do I!"

When the café closed for the night, we would move our *tertulia* to my room at the boardinghouse, where I often played until three or four in the morning. Only a few of the music lovers in the group would have the stamina to stay to the end.

Corvino, the café violinist, joined us there one night. He was also the second violinist of the Madrid Symphony. To say that he was Aragonese is also to say he was open, loyal, and stubborn. He listened to me play, and suddenly the guitar was a revelation to him. He made me repeat whole pieces and difficult or expressive passages.

"Tomorrow afternoon I want to introduce you to Maestro Arbós," he declared. "No one could help you more. If he should like you, he can recommend you to the provincial music groups and to people abroad, if you decide to travel outside of Spain. Meet me after the concert, at the stage door."

This was a blessing. I was running out of funds and spending sleepless nights worrying about it, especially when someone at the *Café de Levante* would point out some bedraggled painter, poet, or writer and say; "See that man in the corner? That toast and coffee he is so avidly swallowing is his only meal for the day!" Or when someone else added; "He won't come near me again. He's already borrowed from me too many times, and knows he won't get any more!" The prospect of being reduced to borrowing or having to eat only a piece of bread a day, made me shudder. My thoughts would turn as black as pitch at the very idea.

When Corvino spoke about introducing me to Arbós my hopes were raised again. Arbós was the high priest of the Spanish music world; he approved or condemned without appeal, beginners, seasoned musicians, composers, newspaper critics, theatrical managers. In our Spanish eyes his small head was hallowed by fame. Rightly so, too. Having finished studying under Monasterio, Queen Maria Cristina had sent him to Brussels to continue the violin under Vieuxtemps and composition under Gevaert. Later it was refreshing to compare the austerity of what Gevaert taught with Arbós's frothy compositions, the best of which is a pyrotechnical sassy tango for violin; it may also be his only piece destined to be remembered.

I slept on and off that night. In the morning Mariana came to wake me.

"*Señorito,* you've overslept! It's ten o'clock and your guitar is silent."

"What's that you have there?" I asked, pointing to something she held in her hand.

"A perfumed letter. My, it does smell good!"

"Give it to me!"

I smiled as I opened it. It was from Maria Querol. Mariana was watching me, I could see her out of the corner of my eye.

"A boy brought it," she broke in, "and, can you believe it, he wanted an answer right away! I told him the *señorito* was still asleep and that I didn't dare wake him up because he would get mad and probably throw something at me. He'll come back tomorrow for his answer."

"Why did you send him away?" I shouted at her. "You're a liar, Mariana; you know I always get up early and in a good mood, too."

"Oh, *señorito,* now you're mad at me. I was only joking. I told the boy to wait downstairs."

Maria Querol was inviting me to tea at her uncle's house that afternoon, and I quickly accepted. Frankly, I had been thinking of her often.

Two such good strokes of luck in one day was like champagne for my blood. I got so nervous I could neither work nor read; I jumped from idea to idea and felt more like enjoying myself than working hard. I took my happiness to the streets to breathe the subtle air of the Castilian plateau which invigorates the body and cheers the spirit, to drink in the May sun or, if it were too strong, to enjoy the fresh humid shade of the sidewalks. This day was to be a feast for my senses, a joy for my heart.

Madrid in those days was cheerful and *simpático.* The compact buildings of today have changed the face of European cities and Madrid has suffered more than most. The steady stream of cars flowing down the streets of Alcalá, the Prado and the Castellana, swirling about the Puerta del Sol and the

Plaza de la Cibeles, seems to get even deeper in the narrower streets; people rush along piling up at the crosswalks until the policeman lets them dash across to the other side of the torrent. All this boiling mass of cars and humanity has taken away our perspective of space and even the time we need to enjoy the city.

How different was my Madrid! More carriages than cars and, in the heat of the early afternoon, more carriages at the hack stands than on the street; all cared for by talkative coachmen who got their poor nags to move with a mixture of invective and endearments, clacking their tongues and snapping their whips.

People came out for the leisurely adventure of their daily walk, to pass the time, always eager to start a conversation on any pretext, ready to forget the very time and place of an appointment. The colorful street vendors hawked their lottery tickets, trinkets, flowers, newspapers, magazines, their voices raised over the shouts of their competitors, filling the crystal air with their chants and cries. Young girls promenaded in their typical Madrileña shawls, their walk provoking ardent male looks amid a chorus of compliments and sighs.

Today the sound of engines and horns has drowned out the cheerful murmur of city life, turning its polychromed sound into a strident monochord lacking in all human vibration. People can only rush about their business; when on foot, they are intent on the problem of not getting run over or crushed to death on a bus; luckier ones crouch over in a car, from which they can barely see through narrow window slits. There are more passersby than strollers. The greeting of a chance friend is brief and impatient. But, who meets friends in the streets these days? It is more like finding a needle in the proverbial haystack. The mania for travel, too, fills the cities with strangers, particularly in summer, and we don't recognize anyone.

As a friend in Córdoba put it, "Nowadays the traveler has to trust his travel log a lot more than his memories or his perceptions. The other day," my Andalusian friend continued, "I saw a foreign lady consult her schedule. Suddenly she exclaimed, 'It's Friday! Then . . . this must be Córdoba!'"

15

Francisco Tárrega

My story takes us now from Madrid to Valencia, omitting the trials and privations which plagued my last five months in the Spanish capital. I lack the craft—or the heart—to crowd in a few sentences the memories and feelings that overtake me when I look back upon those days. It is difficult for me to prune the spontaneous growth generated by this narrative and leave it like those geometric formal gardens which seem to wake up well-shaven every morning. I wish I could do as the poet who wrote a two-verse madrigal to his beloved and sent it with this postscript: "Forgive me, my lady, I did not have the time to make it shorter."

And so . . . to Valencia.

I bought a third-class ticket and took the train for the city where the loving memory of Tárrega lived in the heart of friends, pupils, and fans, the last ones more interested in the instrument than in music, as I soon discovered. It was curious to see the zeal with which all of them—the pupils for their personal narrow view of the issue, the others for no apparent reason—adhered blindly to the method prescribed by the master in his last years: to pluck solely with the finger pads, avoiding contact of the fingernail with the strings . . . to the detriment of the full rendering of the guitar's characteristic qualities: variety of tone color and of sound volume.

Since I was known to belong to the group of the heretics, I surmised I wouldn't be welcome in Tárrega's circle of admirers. Actually, it was my terrible financial situation that had induced me to try my luck in Valencia. It was the only city that had often opened its doors to the master; there his pupils could play in public without risking the critics' old disparaging remarks about the "anti-flamenco" guitar.

Shortly after my arrival I was taken to a Señor Loscos's cigar store, a sort of votive chapel of the Tárregaphiles. Señor Loscos himself knew nothing about music and seldom went to concerts, but his admiration for Tárrega was unbounded. He had never failed to go to the master's financial aid, and he did so discreetly and generously as well as frequently; Tárrega's had been mostly an impoverished life. True, the delicate sensitivity of his art and his kindly disposition fully justified his followers' concern and affection.

The father of a friend of mine in Madrid had provided me with letters of introduction both to Señor Loscos and Father Corell in Valencia. Before reading his through, Loscos thought it wise to temper my hopes.

"It is extremely difficult to find an audience in Valencia for a guitarist who was not a pupil of Tárrega's," he told me.

"But I didn't have the good fortune of knowing him," I said by way of apology, already dismayed at the poor prospects.

Other friends were arriving. Soon we were invited into a large room at the back of the store, where the master used to stop to rest and often played for his friends. I was shown the armchair where he would take a brief siesta after lunch and the straight-backed chair he sat on when he played. I was very moved.

Father Corell arrived and read his letter with pleasure. Tárrega had dedicated his beautiful *Prelude in D Minor* to this priest and that, more than his clerical garb, accounted for the friendship and respect I already felt for him. Courteous, intelligent, wise in the ways of the confessional, he immediately subjected me to a thorough questioning regarding my background, birth, age, family, studies, culture, musical education and, without pausing for breath, about my religious beliefs and practices. All in discreet and pleasant tones, of course. At the conclusion, however, I could not resist the temptation to bow reverently and ask; "Father, your absolution, please . . . or do I have to say my penance first?"

That elicited general laughter and a quiet, friendly sign from the priest. "We would like to hear you play," he said.

Señor Loscos handed me one of two guitars lying on the sofa, one made by García. The other, a better one, a Torres, no doubt, was being reserved for a Tárrega disciple, a "non-nail" guitarist.

I ran through a few chords, scales, and arpeggios just to warm up and get acquainted with the fingerboard.

"You must have very soft nails," mused Father Corell. "Your tone is not metallic."

"Hum!" Loscos reproved him.

"Since you are so well acquainted with the orthodox interpretation of the master's works, allow me to offer something new," I told them, "my own transcription of Debussy's *Second Arabesque.*"

They seemed surprised and a little displeased. However, I went ahead with that tour de force, whose difficulties become diabolical when transferred to the intricate technique of the guitar. No matter; my young fingers seemed to fly as if they had wings, weaving every note without a fault.

When I finished, I looked up and saw that all eyes were fixed on my hands, but no one said a word. Only Father Corell ventured a hushed "Bravo!" and that was greeted, with a frown, by utter silence. Those submusical amateurs didn't like that music. They probably would have preferred a passage from some current zarzuela.

I stood up and no one moved or spoke. After saying

good-bye to Father Corell I left without looking back. No one paid attention to my sudden departure; only a Señor Balaguer and his son Rafael joined me out in the street.

I felt deeply wounded. Had Tárrega been there, I thought, he would never have treated me with such hostility. I was also terribly worried about my crucial financial situation. I knew no one in Valencia and had hardly enough funds to pay for my lodgings. My prospects were blacker than ever.

I heard Señor Balaguer say next to me, "Don't lose heart, kid. We'll see what can be done for you in this town. First, we must get advice from the Iturbi family. I think that what you play has a lot more to do with music than the kind of guitar those meaningless amateurs like. Come to my house for dinner and we'll talk it over."

And talk we did. I soon struck up a friendship with Rafael, his son, a serious, intelligent chap who had a certain flair for the guitar. If his technique was weak and elemental, his playing was not mechanical, and he showed good taste and musical understanding.

16

THE FOLLOWING AFTERNOON the Balaguers came to my boardinghouse on Lauria Street ahead of the friends they had invited to meet me, hear me play and, if they liked me, help me out.

Among the first to arrive were Señor Roca and his daughter. She had been Tárrega's last student—a girl of twenty more graced by her youth than by good looks, whose slight figure lacked feminine softness. She had also been shortchanged in sensitivity and musical perception: her fast, flexible small fingers played the most intricate exercises with amazing speed and accuracy, but without the slightest expression, shading or dynamics. It was like listening to an automated guitar: mere technique.

Her father was a compulsive talker, but I didn't find him overbearing. It was easy to see that he put little stock in his daughter's artistic aspirations, which made his incessant chatter all the more bearable and even amusing. He certainly was not the proverbial father of a prodigy, that tiresome specimen who can become ridiculous when his offspring is no prodigy at all.

Amparo Iturbi and her mother joined us, too. Señora de Iturbi was short and plump, and her facial features seemed somehow out of kilter, but her spontaneous, lively conversation could become quite pleasant if one paid her enough attention and made her feel at ease. Amparo had inherited some of her mother's facial disproportion, but in her case the effect was considerably softened. Her youthful élan and sincere cordiality, the half-candid half-teasing smile always on her lips and, above all, the passionate love of music she exuded, made her gracious and attractive. One sought her company for its lively elegance, and remembered it later with delight.

Amparo was working hard and successfully at her last year of piano studies, awaiting the expert guidance of her brother, José Iturbi. He was about to graduate at the Paris Conservatory and news of his professors' predictions of a first prize and a brilliant future had already reached Valencia.

Finally Father Corell's gentle knock was heard on the door; he had brought along a well-known violin teacher whose name, I am sorry to say, I can't recall.

After much general conversation, all eyes turned to me. I took my Ramírez from its velvety case and played for them.

That gathering brought about the miracle I had been praying for. Señor Roca got ready to pour his exultant loquacity on his friend, the president of the local cultural club, and convince him to sponsor a recital, by me, of course, for the club members. With her mother's consent, Amparo offered to introduce me without delay to Don Eduardo López Chavarri, a former judge and now one of the editors and chief music critic of *Las Provincias*. With his prestigious position on the board of directors of the club, he would reinforce Señor Roca's attack in that direction. The violinist, who had been very favorably impressed with my playing, would line up his fellow musicians and his students to insure, if necessary, a full house for the event. As the promoter of all this goodwill on my behalf, Señor Balaguer was joyfully rubbing his hands. At last Father Corell gave his blessing to the whole enterprise.

Three days later, Rafael gave me the good news: everything was turning out as planned. Thanks to those good friends, the board of directors of the club had fixed a fee of three hundred *pesetas* for the concert, at that time quite a respectable sum for a young artist. Also, an early date had been set for my performance, so I wouldn't have to tighten my belt further.

The turn of events revived my spirits. To the satisfaction of my friends and my tranquility, I regained my usual expansive and contagious optimism.

17

As USUAL, at my Valencian pension, too, I made friends among my fellow boarders. There was Don Prudencio, a retired cavalry major; Don Pepe, a traveling salesman—kitchenware—who was forever boasting about his skirt-chasing adventures; and Don Julián, an intelligent and likable professor of psychology who taught at the local institute.

My old and my new friends would gather around my guitar, actually to spin stories rather than to hear me play. Don Pepe was relentless in his tales of amorous conquests. He resented the jokes and puns he drew from his audience, particularly Don Julián's truly witty ones. Even the presence of Father Corell at our gatherings wouldn't inhibit his shoddy ribaldry. One day, as we talked of things well removed from the theme of his obsession, he interrupted with his usual sally: "Fellows, I had a marvelous time yesterday. What a woman!"

This time Don Julián stopped him there. "Come now, Don Pepe, admit that you get a bigger kick from telling about it than doing it. You are beginning to sound like a professional Casanova I once knew. This man waged a raging battle for a certain lady's heart—although he was aiming at winning something lower down, of course. Anyway, he succeeded at last, and the moment the act had been consummated, he jumped out of bed and began to throw on his clothes. Amazed and disappointed, the woman asked, 'Darling, what's this? Where are you going?' 'To tell my friends about it,' replied the Don Juan as he rushed out the door."

Although less presumptuous than Don Pepe, our retired cavalry major also contributed to our chats. He delighted us and himself with accounts of battles in which he had participated during Spain's unfortunate Rif wars in Africa, pointing out the contradiction between his name, Prudencio, and the bold courage he could muster in the face of the enemy.

". . . And don't think I didn't tremble with terror just before an attack. I would even get furious and insult myself in an effort to snap out of it. Just like that French marshal—what's his name—who would tell himself; 'Ah, you old bag of bones! Trembling again, eh? Just watch and see where I'm going to dump you this time,' and off he'd go with his men to the firing line. Well, I did something like it. The whole battalion would follow me, electrified by my courage. General Aguilera himself believed in it enough to entrust some of his most dangerous operations to me. Yes, the little game almost cost me my life several times."

I gave my concert in Valencia, made my fee and even got some good reviews. In his, López Chavarri referred extensively to Tárrega and his disciples and very little to my performance and my program. However, through Amparo Iturbi, I later learned that in private conversation journalist Chavarri had praised my courage in bypassing the guitar's hackneyed repertoire and playing instead works by Debussy, Tchaikowsky and other "strangers" to this instrument, then. His only regret, he had said, was that such works were transcriptions and not original compositions for the guitar.

Some ten years later, when López Chavarri learned that famous Spanish, French, Polish, and Italian composers were writing works for my guitar, he decided to try his luck and sent me a sonata based on Valencian themes. It was the work of a rank amateur without technical skills or gift for composition, poorly structured, lacking in harmonies. I couldn't help thinking of Fontenelle, the eighteenth-century French scientist, and his wistful remark at his own blind musical spot: *"Sonate, que me veux tu?"* "Sonata, what have you against me?" I put Señor Chavarri's piece aside, winning from him a grudge he held against me until his death at the age of ninety-some years.

After my concert in the city of Valencia, I played once more, in a small nearby town. Although the fee was small, the recital added a little to my purse and a lot to my optimism.

I could not leave the province without visiting Valencia's famous orange groves. A friend of Father Corell's got his *tartana*, his typical Valencian carriage, ready to satisfy my wish; his name was Señor Gil and he did more than that for me: he was kind and generous enough to make me the gift I most prized, books. He gave me over twenty volumes of essays, poetry and fine fiction by French and English authors in Spanish translations, and a few Spanish originals. In my leisure hours I devoured Anatole France's *The Island of Penguins*, Stendhal's *The Charterhouse of Parma*, *Sentimental Journey* by Sterne, and the works of Spaniards like Clarín, Valera, Palacio Valdés and others. I could not be grateful enough for the spiritual solace that Señor Gil's gift provided me with. To boot, I owed him also many hours of instructive and pleasant conversation during my very successful stay in Valencia.

One early morning we left on our tour of the beautiful countryside, already feeling the heat of summer although we were still in the month of May. We drove through vast expanses of rice fields dotted here and there by patches of garden produce and flower orchards. From the latter, I was told, came the "ammunition" for the traditional flower battles that take place, from float to float, in Valencia's famous carnival. There were over twenty million orange trees in those groves, three-quarters of whose crop was destined for foreign markets. As a "distinguished visitor," at one stop in our tour I was introduced to the grandson of the president of the Water Tribunal, a self-governing provincial body which, since the time of the Moors, regulates the irrigation canals that earned Valencia's coastal plane the title of the Garden of Spain.

After a long walk through the groves, we went to the nearby home of a friend of Señor Gil's. There they awaited us with a traditional, succulent *paella,* the aromatic steam gently rising from the seasoned rice. The old-gold hue of the grains reminded me of the warm tones of Titian's nudes, while brushstrokes of red pimentos and green beans added a polychromed variety to the "painting." Good Spanish cooks say, "Food must first get to you through your eyes." In this case, the aroma completed the picture and alerted the palate to the feast ahead. He who is served a good dish of *paella* will desire nothing else—unless he is a troglodyte. That certainly applied to the *paella* of that day.

A light wine, peaceful company and a good digestion soon induced us to take an unscheduled siesta. When we woke up it was time to start the journey back to the city. My visit to the Valencian countryside was too brief and incomplete. It left me with a longing to return and explore further that wondrous garden of Spain, where flowers have the scent of women, women intoxicate like wine, and wine can warm you up faster—and better—than the sun.

I cannot close this chapter on Valencia without recalling the remark of witty writer-monologist Federico García Sanchiz in a letter he once wrote to me from the United States:

"I am now traveling through the countryside around Los Angeles, admiring the vast, well-tended orange groves. Each tree is provided with its own heating unit against frost and protected with who knows what antibiotic dose. I have come to the conclusion that California is a sort of pasteurized Valencia."

Miguel Llobet

THE DAY BEFORE I was to return to Córdoba via Madrid, I was given some news which made me change my plans: Miguel Llobet would be arriving soon in Valencia to stay for a few days. What else could I do but postpone my leave and meet him?

Llobet was Tárrega's star pupil. His prestige was further enhanced by the eminent friends he made while living in Paris; Ravel, Debussy, and Fauré had heard him play and admired him as an interpreter and as an artist. He was a frequent guest of Albéniz and an intimate friend of Granados, whom he often visited in Barcelona. And what made me feel still closer to him: Llobet was not an advocate of the "finger pad" school which condemns plucking the strings with reinforcement from the fingernail. That rebellion had caused him the secret animosity of the dauphin and his followers; it also accounted for some viperlike hisses heard at his recitals. His artistic repute, however, tempered his detractors considerably.

There were no recitals in sight for me, so I thought it wise to conserve what I had earned in Valencia. I moved from the pension in Lauria Street to more modest lodgings and also made sure that my return railroad ticket was valid for a later date. I was afraid of being stranded in Valencia.

I went with Llobet's friends to meet him at the station. I couldn't take my eyes off him from the moment he arrived. He was over middle height, lean, with undistinguished features save for a penetrating, inquisitive look in his eyes. He had a high-pitched voice and an easy laugh which often ended in sopranolike giggles. He wore clean but ill-fitting clothes, without the affectations adopted by some artists—myself included, although in my case the purpose was not to attract the attention of the common herd but rather to isolate myself from it. Llobet had not let his hair grow into a mane, nor did he wear a flowing cravat or a floppy black fedora. He looked, in short, like any businessman of modest means.

As we shook hands he said to me, "My friends in Madrid and Seville have praised you highly in their letters."

"They are just being kind," I replied. "You'll soon have a chance to discover my faults. I haven't worked within the master's school—I had to devise my own technique."

He smiled and we parted, as friends took him away to the home where he was to stay during his visit in Valencia. The Balaguers, who stayed behind with me, told me that all of us would meet at their home the next day at six o'clock.

Every friend and fan of the guitar was there next day, myself, like everyone else, burning to hear Llobet play. But to the surprise and consternation of all, he refused to play. He was too tired, he said, after the trip . . . from Barcelona to Valencia! Needless to say, his negative attitude created a very bad impression. We tried to cover up our surprise and disappointment and conversation veered off awkwardly into meaningless chatter. He did not ask me to play nor did anyone else suggest it. No other guitar but his was to be heard that night among us, a commendable gesture of loyalty and respect.

Llobet himself broke off the gathering an hour later. He

invited everyone to meet again at some other house the next day, when he promised he would play for us.

And there we were next day, frozen into the most reverent attention. My heart pounded with excitement when he at last reached for his Torres guitar. He opened with the prelude that Tárrega had dedicated to him. Without a pause, ignoring the signs and sounds of admiration which greeted that first piece, he went right into a Mendelssohn *Romance* he had recetly transcribed for the guitar and which he played with zest and passion. That was followed with a Chopin prelude, and he closed the first part of the program with Bach's *bourrée in B minor* in Tárrega's transcription.

Everyone stood up; some went over to embrace him, others to express their delight with silent gestures. I waited my turn and then approached him quietly. I took one of his hands in both of mine and pressed it warmly, while I told him softly what a great artist he was, great among the finest violinists, cellists, pianists . . . I remember mentioning Cortot. . . . No other guitarist I had heard, I told him, had made me forget the limitations of the guitar or revealed the scope of its potential. I assured him I agreed implicitly with his technique and would follow it relentlessly, no matter how difficult the path ahead for me. . . .

Pleased, I thought, he gave me one of his soprano giggles and got ready to play again. This time he began with his transcription of two *Dances* by Granados. And then he played *El Mestre*, the most beautiful of Catalan songs which Llobet harmonized and scored for the guitar. The effective "orchestration" of its tone color and its delicious dissonances play on the plaintive character of that folk theme, "My teacher has fallen in love with me . . ." making it one of the priceless jewels of the guitar repertoire. Even today, as I write this in the mid-seventies, I still love it as I did then.

"When will I hear you play?" he asked me as we parted that night.

"Come to lunch with me tomorrow and I'll play for you," I answered, already planning to ignore those aficionados of Tárrega's most inconsequential bagatelles. "Let's have only the

Balaguers and Father Corell with us, if you will. They are not musicians, but they do appreciate robust fare."

After hearing Miguel Llobet play several times, I gathered the following impressions:

First, his technique was far from being the feat which so impressed both musicians and laymen at that time. The musicians attributed his effects to the magic of virtuosity because they probably had not yet heard polyphonic music played on the guitar; and the laymen would raise their hands in awe the moment they heard fast scales executed smoothly on any instrument. Actually, without being extraordinary, Llobet's technique was excellent. I did notice that he always faltered in the same passages, even in relatively easy ones—probably because of lack of discipline or more likely due to laziness (as I later found out, he was lazy, indeed). He could gloss over the most difficult positions and the fastest progression of notes with his "soapy" fingering.

Second, his tone was rasping and metallic, lacking in roundness, volume and resilience. The followers of the dauphin (Tárrega) would glance maliciously at one another when he tore grating sounds from the strings with his fingernails.

Third, he was undoubtedly a good musician and a great artist, a serious, noble interpreter of Bach whose music he played with controlled feeling, crisp rhythms, and firm accents. He allowed himself a more passionate romanticism in the works of Schumann, Mendelssohn and Schubert. However, he was less temperamentally suited to understanding and feeling the characteristic works of Albéniz and Granados.

Catalonia has been the birthplace or training ground of great artists of varying sensitivity. Among them, Albéniz had no peer in capturing the very essence of Andalusian art. And yet, to that art he owed but one or two specific themes of his vast and varied output. Other composers and interpreters were by nature indifferent to the beauty and elegance, the rhythmic intricacies, the poetry and feeling of the folklore inherent to my glorious Andalusia. Llobet belonged in this last group.

It is a shame that echoes of his great talent were not

faithfully recorded. What records he was persuaded to make are worthless and should be destroyed as an act of respect for him and his memory.

In spite of the difference in our ages, Llobet and I became good friends and, in time, the results of our relationship were happy ones for me. My attitude towards him was one of admiration for the artist and affection for the friend. Once he had tested my technique and capacity of expression, his esteem for me was probably increased by my profound determination to broaden the guitar's repertoire and raise the instrument's prestige. I was in every sense a friend!

The first development in our growing friendship was his invitation to follow him to Barcelona. I accepted eagerly, of course. Together we left Valencia. We talked extensively on the train, getting better acquainted both artistically and personally. In deference to his age and renown, I tried to let him do most of the talking. He promised to help me start getting around in Barcelona by introducing me to some influencial music circles, but he certainly did not commit himself in two very important steps for me: an introduction to Granados, and some recommendation that could lead to my giving a recital or a "club" concert in the Catalonian capital, any public performance that would help relieve my chronic lack of funds.

"Well-known foreign artists play frequently in Barcelona," he told me. "Sometimes there are two or three such concerts in a week. Not so in the case of Spanish artists, not even Catalonians. Except, an occasional performance by Casals and once in a great while, and with much less success, one by Manén."

I was surprised to learn that he himself had never played in public in Barcelona, his native city. I found it even stranger that in his ten years in Paris he had given only one recital, and that, sharing the program with a mediocre pianist.

"Why?" I ventured.

"Concert halls are too large, and the guitar doesn't have the power to carry sound from the stage to the entire hall. The audience has to strain itself to hear us, listeners become impatient. Then too, we don't have enough works of universal appeal to satisfy the concert public and the reviewers."

It wasn't easy for me to accept that disparaging appraisal of the guitar's potential; but, if anything, those words reinforced my determination to seek the cooperation of serious composers and help enrich the repertoire of our much-neglected beautiful instrument. Moreover, those words convinced me at last that Spain's most notable luthiers had to be encouraged to search for means of increasing the volume of the guitar without electrical or artificial devices. Suddenly I recalled how miraculously my guitar was heard on both banks of the wide Guadalquivir one night when a group of friends and I went on a "lyrical-fluvial" excursion in a fishing barge.

I couldn't have been too far off then in my expectations. In sixty years of playing concerts everywhere, my guitar has been heard, to the satisfaction of my listeners and without electrical amplification, in halls seating at times up to five thousand people.

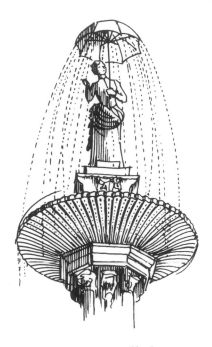

19

SHORTLY BEFORE OUR TRAIN pulled into Barcelona, Llobet, who prided himself on being very neat, took out a clothes brush from his satchel and proceeded to dust off his suit, hat and raincoat. He then produced a well-used chamois and began to shine his shoes. To my astonishment, he also wiped his walking cane. Thinking it was a joke, I burst out laughing, but he didn't crack a smile and continued his operation until he was fully satisfied with his appearance.

His wife, young daughter, and brother awaited him on the platform. I liked his brother right away; he seemed to be both a composed and a practical man. He shook hands with me and immediately relieved his brother of satchel and guitar case. I could not say the same for Señora de Llobet. Nothing but bitterness was reflected in her face; she hardly allowed a smile to surface when I greeted her—a tall, dry-thin, withdrawn woman. The daughter, on the other hand, already showed signs of a plumpness which was to grow into obesity some years later.

As we parted at the station, Llobet asked me to go to his home and fetch him the following afternoon around six o'clock.

I took a room in a dark and dingy pension on Conde de Asalto street; it gave onto a small inner courtyard and was so wrapped in gloomy shadows that the low-watt bare bulb hanging from the ceiling had to be switched on day and night. The place was so depressing, it filled me with such pessimism and despair, that I almost cried just thinking of my uncle's amiable, sunny little villa in Granada. The owner asked for a week's lodgings in advance, but I refused to comply and said I would pay daily every morning before breakfast. He agreed. As he left me alone in that room, I was tempted to ask him if the previous tenants had been cattle or horses.

Llobet's apartment, too, was not cheerful. The stairwell to his floor was narrow, steep, and dark as a tunnel. The sun graced his living room only briefly and on the slant. The furniture couldn't have been in worse taste; the only relief in that living room was a narrow balcony facing the street. There was a small oil by Zuloaga on the largest wall, but that was engulfed in an ugly collection of family photographs and a few prints.

An upright piano displayed its yellow teeth which, in color, if not in number, resembled those of the mistress of the house. The good lady played it often, stumbling through fragments of classic and romantic pieces, pausing to mumble her regret at having given up a musical career for marriage. Apparently her husband's artistic prestige did not appease her nostalgia.

My first outing with Llobet in Barcelona was to the dairy barn of León Ferré where Tárrega's pupils and guitar fans congregated, much as they did in Valencia at Loscos' cigar store. Milk was sold to the public in the front of the store, separated from the cowshed in the back by a thick curtain. The cows' lowing and mooing echoed in the cavity of the guitar, distorting whatever the officiating fan was playing at the time. The owner, León Ferré, an extremely generous and friendly man, offered his large group of guitar friends all manner of pastries, cookies and puddings to be washed down with enormous glasses of fresh milk. It could be that those delicious snacks accounted for the considerable attendance and frequency of those gatherings.

Llobet introduced me to Señor Ferré in glowing terms, although he did worry me a bit with repeated references to my "lightning speed." Ferré was most courteous and invited me to play.

I tuned my guitar one tone higher—I had to compete with those cows!—and then rode my battle pony: Debussy's *Second Arabesque*. Llobet, who by then had heard me play it several times, turned to the others at the end and exclaimed in Catalan: "What skill! What skill!"

The son of our host the milkman was a sensitive violinist. He offered to take me to the home of the Cassadó family, whose son, Gaspar, was a talented cellist and a very cordial chap, he said. "I think you two will be good friends," he added.

I wanted so much to ask Llobet for copies of Granados' *Dances* and *El Mestre*. But I remembered how Fortea in Madrid had denied my request for other transcriptions. I was wrong. Llobet was different. When I did muster the courage to broach the subject timidly, he answered immediately, "Actually, I haven't written down those works yet. But, why don't you come to my home in the mornings and learn them from me? Bring your guitar. I'll play the pieces on mine and pass the music on to you, phrase by phrase. What do you think?"

What did I think? I jumped to my feet, embraced him, and said, "Thank you . . . thank you. . . ."

I was not alone with Llobet at those sessions. Friends of his, guitar aficionados and would-be teachers, witnessed the transfer of those works, segment by segment. Among them was one Sirera, a croupier at a local gambling house, who had been taking lessons from the dauphin and getting advice from

Segovia at the age of twenty-five. Barcelona.

Llobet, none of which seemed to have made much of a dent in his stubborn mediocrity. He and another guitarist tried to benefit from those sessions and attempted to do what Llobet was showing me. They soon gave up when they realized that they could neither follow the maestro's fingers nor memorize the sequence of musical phrases, forcing poor Llobet to repeat every passage and fingering to exhaustion. During those endless repetitions I would sit away from the group and quietly go over what I had just learned. I never gave a sign of impatience or said anything which might have slighted them; nevertheless, Sirera took a violent dislike to me. I paid no mind; in less than ten days I memorized the two dances and a *tonadilla* by Granados, and *El Mestre*, which I loved so much. I felt I was in heaven.

My gratitude and affection for Llobet increased progressively, and not only for his time and generosity in teaching me those transcriptions—a priceless gesture—but also because I was aware of his heroic patience in withstanding his nagging wife's daily reproaches, quarrels and complaints.

The young violinist, the milkman's son, presented me to the Cassadó family. They had a piano store on the Paseo de Gracia, one of Barcelona's main streets, and lived above it in the same building.

Señora de Cassadó was a sturdy and energetic woman whose authoritarian voice and manner seemed to proclaim: "Beware! No one gets the better of me!"

The husband, much the same in size and looks, was nevertheless her total opposite in temperament: a friendly, sweet smiling man. He always wore a cutaway when he went out, unaware that the garment did not lend him the dignity he sought but, on the contrary, made him look ridiculous. The trunk of his body was that of a good-sized, hefty man, but his legs had not developed proportionately. To boot, his bushy beard and droopy moustache gave him the look of a wise, kindly old gnome.

If my memory does not fail me, Joaquín Cassadó, with or without cutaway, was the organist in a church in the Gracia section of the city. I was told that, besides several works for orchestra, piano, and string ensembles, he had composed an opera entitled *El Monje Negro (The Black Monk)* which every year the Liceo Theater would promise to include in "the next season's repertoire." I wonder if it ever did get performed, but it was touching to see the feverish anxiety with which the family awaited its premiere.

I cannot judge the merit of his compositions; I only heard one called *Lo Titi*, a light piece he had written for Gaspar, his son, the cellist, but when the talented young fellow played it as an encore in his concerts, it made me realize how misguided filial love can be at times.

I, too, was graced by Cassadó with a composition for the guitar, an *allegro appassionato* which suited neither my instrument nor my taste. It is still on my shelf of forgotten music.

Gaspar, the oldest of the Cassadós' four children, had been endowed with genuine musical talent. He had chosen the cello, which to me is the noblest of instruments after the guitar; it can produce beautiful, manly tones, and if its highest notes do not always ring true, in the middle and lower registers it can express passion with more depth and eloquence than any other instrument.

Although the characteristics of the cello do not lend themselves to a display of technique as fluidly as the violin, Gaspar Cassadó, as Casals—and I know whereof I speak—possessed a miraculous flexibility in both hands. His left, without the slightest effort, glided over the fingerboard, overcoming technical intricacies with the greatest of ease. Meanwhile, his bow would respond to his commands as if it were an extension of his right hand. On those technical qualities he based the richest, most effective musical sense I have observed in a musician throughout my life.

Perhaps the circumstances of growing up in a musical milieu helped develop in this case a precocious talent that was more intuitive than cultivated. The father had neglected his son's musical education, but with his penetrating instinct, Gaspar was able to prevail over the most difficult problems of technique and interpretation.

Frankly, he played like an angel. I was profoundly moved when I first heard him. His tone was sweet, full, pure, lacking in the unmusical rasping often produced by the bow in passages of great stress and strength. If his volume was not very powerful then, it probably was because he had not yet been smitten with ambition to achieve greater success in larger halls. I still remember the first piece he played for me, Fauré's *Élégie*, beautifully accompanied by a young pianist. I shall never forget that thrill.

Naturally, I had to play for him—and for his family. One night I brought my guitar over to their house. When time came to get ready to play, I looked around for a stool or some appropriate object on which to place my left foot. Señora Cassadó remembered that the family had a proper footstool somewhere. She went to fetch it, and when she returned with it, I exclaimed, "It's perfect!"

Always the businesswoman, right then and there she replied: "If you like it, I can let you have it at a reasonable price."

How that disconcerted me! What could I say? If I accepted, I'd have to spend my scant money in something I didn't need, and if I refused, I risked offending her.

Gaspar came to the rescue. "Mother, please," he said, "we want to hear him play!"

Gaspar and I met almost daily and developed a fine friendship. Because he was a Catalan and well liked by his father's influential friends but, above all, because of his cordiality and open friendliness, some of Barcelona's fine families had opened their doors to him. It was typical of Gaspar that, through him, they should also be opened to me, his friend.

As always, I was plagued by my acute penury. One day I approached Llobet and suggested that he speak to his brother, a member of the board of directors of the Fine Arts Club. Perhaps he could arrange a recital for me at one of the club's halls. Llobet agreed to speak to his brother—while I caught a glimpse of his wife's displeasure reflected in her look.

When news reached me that the arrangements for my recital were on the way, I went to consult with Llobet about my program. I was anxious to include the transcriptions I had recently learned from him. His wife, who actually had never addressed me directly, this time met me face to face.

"Those works shouldn't be heard in public unless my husband plays them first," she told me.

More astonished by the bitterness in her voice than by her words, I replied, "You are right, *señora*. I promise never to play them without first getting your permission. If you prefer, I'll start forgetting them right now."

I bade Llobet good-bye, nodded to his wife, and left them alone to fight it out.

The recital at the Fine Arts Club did take place, but I was doubly frustrated with the results: I received neither fee nor reviews. The organizers had "forgotten" two important details: to notify the members of the club that the event had been scheduled and the date, and to send announcements to the press. I couldn't have given a more private concert! The Cassadó family was there with a few friends and guitar fans, and some members of the club did look in, curious to see what was going on in that hall.

20

If in most ways my recital at the Fine Arts Club had been a disaster, it did give me the opportunity to make one of the most fruitful and lasting friendships of my life.

Among the few guitar friends who went to hear me were Dr. Antonio Quiroga from Galicia and his wife, Paz de Armesto. She had studied under Tárrega, but her incurable shyness made it impossible for her to play in front of anyone outside her closest family. No one else had heard her play, or knew how she played or whether she still played the guitar. What was obvious to anyone interested in the guitar was her deep love and concern for the instrument.

She was not a beautiful woman, but she was a gracious person to meet and to know. That she was the daughter of grandees was evident in her dress, poise, dignity and speech, although there wasn't an ounce of arrogance or affectation in her. Her mother, the daintiest, most delicate woman I had met, was then past seventy, but she so impressed me that one day I thought I'd pay her a compliment: "If I were your age, I would ask you to marry me!"

Dr. Quiroga was a kind, amiable, uncomplicated man. As in the case of other sons of wealthy families at that time, his university studies had been done haphazardly, with more attention paid to adventure stories and popular literature than to medical books, which reminded me of Miguel de Unamuno's remark: "Some doctors kill their patients because they are afraid of letting them die, and some let them die because they are afraid of killing them."

Dr. Quiroga solved the problem simply by giving up his practice. In collaboration with some fellow Galicians and Catalan physicians, he founded a medical products firm, *Laboratorios Puig*, of which, as majority shareholder, he became the director.

At the end of my recital at the Fine Arts Club, the Quirogas stayed to congratulate me and invite me to lunch at their home the following day. I was touched by the spontaneous offer of their friendship and support.

"My mother-in-law has a very fine antenna to judge people on sight," Dr. Quiroga told me smilingly. "When you came in she looked at you, tuned in, and took me aside to whisper that she was sure you were a fine chap, sound of mind and body, and I should make friends with you."

It did not take me long to feel close enough to that charming family to tell them about myself and my work since I had left Córdoba and started to travel—including my quarrel with the "fingerpad" followers of the Tárrega school in Valencia. I even ventured to tell them of Señora de Llobet's hostility, to which I attributed the poor handling of my recital at the Fine Arts Club at the cost to me of both fee and reviews.

In a generous, impulsive gesture, Dr. Quiroga offered to organize another recital for me, this time making the arrangements himself, to take place at one of the salons of his laboratory building, with the proper handling and paid attendance—

which meant that relief was in sight for my injured pride and my dwindling purse.

The recital at *Laboratorios Puig* was admirably handled; there were no "oversights" to deplore. Two large rooms were converted into a concert hall by throwing open the large folding doors separating them. Those two salons were filled by doctors, chemists, pharmacists, nurses, technicians, and all manner of good people connected with the blessed healing arts, together with their wives, husbands, mothers, fathers, brothers, sisters, nephews, nieces, and friends! More than three hundred persons were crowded into those two rooms. Dr. Quiroga beamed proudly at the results of his effort. The guests of honor were Dr. Prats, the current luminary of the Barcelona School of Medicine, and Dr. Guardia, the technical director of *Laboratorios Puig.*

Miguel Llobet was there, of course, without his wife. He sat next to Señora de Quiroga and her seraphic mother, and as both ladies later told me, he would turn to them during the pauses and whisper repeatedly his enthusiastic: "What skill! What skill!" in Catalan. Needless to say, the Cassadó family was there, too, to a man.

I never called again at Llobet's home after my disagreement with his wife over the transcriptions. I would meet him at the home of Dr. Severino García. This man had such monumental vanity and conceit that, lacking enough musical knowledge or scoring technique, he dared retranscribe everything Tárrega already had transcribed for the guitar. Somehow he persuaded the prestigious music publishing house, Dotesio, to publish such sacrileges, and they still can be found in print.

Llobet gave us his latest news: he would soon be leaving with Granados for New York to attend the premiere of *Goyescas* and give some concerts there himself. I held my tongue and did not remind him of my longing to meet Granados. He seemed to have forgotten that old wish of mine, and I surmised that the inducer of the "mental lapse" had been none other than his wife.

114

Señor Cassadó, the father of my cellist friend Gaspar, had arranged for the secretary of the Catalan Chamber Music Society to call at his home on business matters. Once again Gaspar proved his affection for me by suggesting that we take advantage of the occasion to have the influential secretary meet me and hear me play. "Who knows," he said, "maybe he'll schedule you to play at the society this season or next. If he does, it will be a giant step in your career!"

The secretary did hear me play and seemed ready to recommend me to the society's governing board and president. There were, however, some serious obstacles in our path, as Gaspar and I had expected. For one thing, I was not a Catalan, although that could have been overlooked if Llobet had not been in Barcelona then. Because of his age and prestige as well as his Catalan origin, it was only right that he be the first classic guitarist to play for the prestigious society, a group highly regarded in all of Spain. That seemed perfectly logical and correct to me, of course. I understood; had Llobet not been in town it could have been different. . . .

The secretary raised another question: would our delicate instrument be heard at the Palau, the society's concert hall? When consulted, Llobet himself gave an irrevocably adverse answer. "The sound of this poetic instrument is delightful in small, intimate quarters, but in a hall like the Palau, I'm afraid it would vanish into thin air," and on he went with a long dissertation on the subject. He not only closed the doors of the society to me, but also to the guitar.

Nevertheless, through a lucky encounter I found another way. One day, quite accidentally, I met Mateo Fernández de Soto on the street. Mateo was a sculptor and an architect I had met in Córdoba together with his younger brother, Wenceslao, when they were working to restore Trajan's city gate. It had not taken them long to find and join our group: Pepe Chacón, Pedro Antonio Baquerizo, Luis Serrano, and others I have mentioned before.

Mateo was talented and sensitive—and also lazy and negligent. However, he could spring suddenly from the depths of lethargy and burst out into surprising activity. Still, because of his own neglect, his name as a professional was known only to his friends. He had not bothered to obtain the necessary licenses and diplomas, thus many of his admirable architectural projects were signed by and attributed to fellow architects.

I had been closer to Wenceslao, the younger brother; Mateo was quite a few years older. After having lost track of them when I left Córdoba, meeting them now in Barcelona was a delightful surprise.

The brothers introduced me to their *tertulia,* or group of intellectuals, who met daily at the Maison Dorée, a French-type café that used to be where the Banco Central stands now facing Barcelona's main square, the Plaza de Cataluña. Among the regulars in the group were a Señor Ponsa—a wealthy businessman and art lover who was known to sponsor some young painters; Alejandro Riquer, both a painter and a writer; Mariano Andreu, a painter, sculptor and excellent enamelist; Padilla, another painter whose work became highly prized. All of them belonged to Picasso's circle of friends—Mateo was particularly close to him—and were expecting him soon in Barcelona.

I hit it off so well with that crowd that after they heard me play at Riquer's studio they vowed to pool their influential contacts and the goodwill of their friends to make sure I would have a successful concert in Barcelona, one they would organize themselves. The question was: where? We could not hold it in a regular theater or in one of Barcelona's two public concert halls, the Sala Mozart and the Sala Granados; expenses would be too high and not enough tickets would be sold to cover them. After all, I was still unknown.

The Maison Dorée group finally resorted to twisting someone's arm: that of the manager of Galerías Layetana. It was there that I gave my first public concert in Barcelona. To publicize the event, Mariano Andreu designed a striking poster with a drawing he had done of me, in free strokes but an excellent likeness, captioned with my name, the place and date of the recital. Señor Ponsa paid for the printing and distribution of the poster, we saw it on display in the most strategic points of town. Also with the drawing, they printed a clever combination of postcard-ticket, to be sold for the admission price, five *pesetas*, if I remember correctly—about one dollar at that time. The drawing was repeated on the program, for which Alejandro Riquer wrote a flattering presentation note.

Llobet did not attend that recital; he had already left for New York with Granados. His wife, however, accepted the Quirogas' invitation to attend with them. No need to repeat her objections to my technique, interpretations and even my stage presence, all expressed right while I was playing. Since she found no echo in the Quirogas, their friendship with them fell below the freezing point. I could well imagine her displeasure when she read my reviews the next morning, particularly the one I received in Barcelona's *La Vanguardia*. The Catalans, I found, could not have been more cordial and receptive to me, Señora de Llobet notwithstanding.

It was in Barcelona that I gave two concerts that were most significant to me in my private life and my career, as we will see.

Frank Marshall had attended my Galerías Layetana recital. He had been the assistant director of the Granados Academy, now that Granados was away—unfortunately on what was to be his last trip—Marshall had taken over the full directorship of the renowned music school. He was an excellent musician, fine pianist, and dedicated teacher, born in England but Hispanized by the sun, the wines and women of Spain. One of his pupils is the famous and delightful Alicia de Larrocha.

Joaquín Cassadó had introduced us during the intermission, and Marshall told me how much he liked the last part of the recital. At the end, he said he wanted to hear me play again and also discuss with me an idea that had occurred to him while I was playing. Intrigued, I asked Gaspar Cassadó what he thought Marshall had in mind. Gaspar smiled and hesitated and finally said, "I think he'd rather tell you himself, perhaps later when we meet at my house."

I wondered if Marshall wanted to invite me to teach guitar at the Academy.

As planned, we met after the recital at the Cassadós' home. After the music, chatter and laughter of the party died down, Marshall told me quite plainly, "Would you like to give a concert at the Sala Granados?" Without waiting for an answer, he continued, "I can't mention a fixed fee because the hall is in the Bonanova section, a little out of the way to attract much of a crowd, but expenses won't be too high. There is bound to be something left for you." His Anglo-Saxon business caution was showing!

All I yearned to do at that time was to play as often as possible and play for audiences that took music seriously. And now this man was offering me a recital at the Sala Granados, no less! Of course I agreed enthusiastically, whatever the financial outcome.

Right then and there we discussed and selected the program. I can't remember much of it now, but I suppose it consisted of works from my then not too varied or extensive repertoire. However, for sentimental reasons I will explain later, I do remember that I played the *Andante* from Mozart's *Sonata No. 2 in C Major*, transcribed by Tárrega.

An impressive review of my Galerías Layetana recital had appeared in *La Vanguardia*, Barcelona's first newspaper and one of Spain's best. That must have aroused the curiosity of the city's music fans, for the spontaneous public, together with friends invited by the Quirogas, the Cassadós and my Maison Dorée group, filled the Sala Granados.

That concert was a memorable occasion for me for more than one reason. Among the people I received in the adjacent small salon after the concert, was a beautiful young girl of about fifteen; enormous blue eyes, a delicate nose, fine smiling lips, a graceful slim figure, half-child, half-woman . . . a delightful vision. Her mother, portly and elegant, was right behind her. Frank Marshall introduced us. "Paquita Madriguera and her mother, Andrés."

The young girl took my hand in hers. "I just loved the Mozart *andante*," she said enthusiastically. "It sounds marvelous on the guitar."

I had heard of this budding brilliant pianist. The London press and public had raved about her. Although her talent was mature for her years, it seemed to have a solid quality that went beyond the fleeting flash often displayed by child prodigies. She had studied with Granados since the age of eight, and she was already an accomplished musician as well as a very promising pianist.

Enthralled, I looked at her, pleased by her flattering words but not quite myself in the presence of such a young person who was already famous in Spain and abroad, while I . . .

In a few weeks Paquita left with her mother for New York. For months I thought of her, time and time again, although I knew well that my work required all my energies and concentration. Whenever I would open the shrine where I kept my memories of her, a mysterious inner voice seemed to tell me softly that she and I were destined to meet frequently in the future and form a close and lasting relationship. Indeed, we did. She became my wife some time later.

If my concert at the Sala Granados was to be of great significance in my personal life, the last one I gave in Catalonia at that period played an important part in the history of the guitar as a concert instrument, something which in turn influenced my career.

I have already mentioned Llobet's categorical opinion regarding the guitar's "inability" to produce enough sound volume to be heard throughout large concert halls. This had also been said by Tárrega and his students. If they, the top exponents of the classical guitar, held such views, who could blame critics, audiences and other musicians for agreeing with them?

I can hardly describe the derision and censure provoked among those simple minds by the announcement of my farewell concert at the Palau. The hall, unless my memory fails me, seated over a thousand persons! Some claimed that conceit had turned my head; others relished the thought of my forthcoming disaster at the vast, venerable hall.

Pujol—not the musicologist, but the managing director of the Palau—arranged to meet with me one afternoon at his office in the same building. By then I had given eleven successful concerts in Barcelona and I told him I hoped to give my farewell performance in the city at the Palau.

"But can the guitar be heard in such a large place?" was his immediate response.

"That we shall see, if you permit me to make a little experiment," I said.

I had brought along Juanito Parra with me. He was a friend more than a student, who sometime later became professor of guitar at the Barcelona Municipal School of Music. I sent him home to fetch my Ramírez.

While we waited for him to return with the guitar, I asked Señor Pujol to stand in various spots of the hall, while I stood in the middle of the stage, snapping my fingers at intervals— much in the way that flamenco dancers and singers call *"tocar pitos."* Each time I would ask Pujol if he could hear me. Yes, he could, he said, as he moved to another spot further back from the stage.

When Parrita (our nickname for Juanito Parra) arrived with my guitar, I asked him to take my place on stage and play, successively, loud and soft chords, arpeggios, basses, trebles, legatos, harmonics, while Pujol took me to the very spots from where he had heard my finger-snapping. That thorough test was highly satisfactory, but I still had one objection.

"The acoustics of the Palau are so good," I said ironically, "that not only the sounds originating in the hall can be heard. The ones coming from outside can be heard in it, too. Would it be possible to post a policeman out on the street to route away noisy traffic? I mean, the shouts of street vendors, children playing, the horns and clatter of passing cars . . ."

He would see what could be done about it, Pujol said, a bit thrown off by the unusual request.

We had agreed that the guitar indeed could be heard in the hall. Now we returned to his office to discuss the financial details of the recital. All I can remember is that they were unfavorable to me. But what did I care? My only obligation was to send some money to my mother whenever I could do so without starving. I accepted the one-sided contract.

As a mere formality, Pujol withheld his final acceptance until he could get the approval of the society's president, but in a few days he called me to say that all was settled and ask me for the program to be sent to the printer's.

Contrary to the dire predictions of the opposition, the

Palau was nearly full for my recital and the surprised audience found that all they needed to do to hear every work I played was to remain silent and attentive. There had been rumors that some extremists were ready to demonstrate against me, but apparently their plans were thwarted in view of the obvious respect and enthusiasm of the general audience.

In a night abounding in emotions, the one that moved me most was the realization that I had broadened the scope of the guitar and proved it *could* be heard from any stage. Concert audiences in the great European halls *could* enjoy the poetry of sound, the richness of orchestral color, the alluring musicality with which Heaven had endowed this instrument to make it the noblest close friend of the human soul.

But alas! Something was still to be accomplished if, as I dreamed, the guitar was to share a stellar place in the music firmament with the violin, the cello, the piano. My kingdom for a repertoire!

21

MOST OF THE MONEY I had been earning in Barcelona I was handing over for safekeeping to my honorary guardian, Dr. Quiroga. I kept only what was absolutely necessary for my daily needs which, at this point, were not too high, since I had most of my meals at the Quirogas' home.

My new prosperity allowed me to change living quarters from the awful, dingy pension on Conde de Asalto to a more attractive one on Fernando Street. Now I had a large room, a balcony facing the street, an ample bed, a wide and sturdy table for my music and my books—the books given to me by that blessed gentleman in Valencia—and an armchair which under different circumstances would have been a sort of seat of torture, but which at this juncture seemed like the height of luxury and comfort.

One day I got to my room and found a couple of young

fellows who had burst into my room during my absence and taken my guitar from its case. One of them was strumming it awkwardly. I was indignant.

"What's this? You have a nerve! Had I known there were such bums in this house I would have locked my door. Get out!"

"We're fellow boarders," they said. "We didn't think you'd mind."

"That's no excuse! How can you know what that instrument means to me? Out, I said!"

I was already reaching for the sturdy water jug on my dresser when they left the room, poor devils, laughing and making fun of me.

When I told the Quirogas of the incident, they immediately offered me the doctor's former office and medical library, which the ladies had converted into a quiet family retreat. Doña Filomena, the mother, Doña Paz, the wife, and Dr. Antonio treated me like a member of their family by then, so I had no qualms in accepting their offer. Thereafter I would work and study in their home and use my room at the pension only as sleeping quarters.

My friend Alejandro Piquer introduced me to Jaume Pahissa, the Catalan composer, who I had heard was not interested in writing for solo instruments or chamber groups. He wanted to compose only for vast orchestral masses. That gift, much admired in Catalan music circles, led me to believe that Pahissa was a titan of a composer. I wondered if the quality of his work—probably influenced by Mahler—justified the use of such mammoth means of expression. Upon meeting him, I was on the verge of apologizing, facetiously, for being an exponent of such minor and negligible music as that produced by the instrument of my specialty. I didn't, of course.

Together with his reputation as a sort of musical whale, Pahissa was also known to be lazy, indolent, and a night owl. He always went to bed at sunrise and rose late in the evening. When did he work? It was said that his income was provided by two generous wealthy men, Cambo and Roviralta, and a banking firm known to help struggling artists.

123

Segovia at the age of twenty-five. Barcelona.

He was a friendly and pleasant man to know; tall, dark, bushy-haired, with small sharp eyes and an open laugh. He seldom made a display of his considerable cultural background and there was no nonsense about his sound and solid aesthetic theories.

The moment we were introduced, Pahissa told me that his friend, Eugenio D'Ors, the renowned Catalan essayist and art critic, had written a commentary about me. The piece was to be published soon in *Veu de Catalunya*, a Barcelona journal. Although I had read little of his work, I knew about the famous writer through my Madrid friends. I was flattered by the prospect of being the subject of one of his articles, and I told Pahissa I would like to thank D'Ors personally.

A few days later the composer sent me a message with the friend who had introduced us, Alejandro Piquer: we were to meet at the Maison Dorée one evening at eleven.

I arrived on the dot, as usual, and as usual, Pahissa was late. I looked around and saw a hand waving at me. It was Eugenio D'Ors, pointing to a seat next to him at his table. "Sit down," he told me smilingly. "He'll find us, if he ever gets here."

I was about to thank him for writing a piece about me, but the moment I mentioned it, he cut me short.

"What do you think of the title, *The Guitar and the Tennis Racket?*"

"Forgive me," I said. "I don't see the connection."

"Both are strung with gut."

"In that case, why not ask the tennis player to make his strings sing, too, as the guitarist?"

Pahissa arrived then and stood over us, waiting for D'Ors to finish his beer. Meanwhile, I was studying the writer's face and expressions. Long, thick eyebrows accented his wide, noble forehead. His eyes reflected a deep intellect, contrasting with his easy laugh and facile humor. His fine, eloquent hands moved in short gestures unlike the sweeping ones made by most Mediterranean people. He spoke slowly, with frequent remarks which, like those of Heine, could be both poetic and ironic. Years later I was to be amazed at how much his voice and speech had changed; he had acquired a kind of *staccato,*

125

musically speaking, a lack of *legato* in his syllables. Miguel de Unamuno used to say that Eugenio D'Ors spoke all languages, including his own, with a foreign accent. All who knew him had the same impression.

As we left the café, D'Ors steered towards the dark little streets and old buildings surrounding the cathedral—those that had survived the demolishing mania of city developers. We strolled through the Gothic section, stopping here and there to hear D'Ors recite a bit of poetry, his own or someone else's. At that time I hardly understood everyday Catalan, let alone the refined literary form he was using.

I tagged along until he and Pahissa realized I was being dragged like a piece of luggage and thus was likely to stay behind and lose them altogether. They then began to translate the ideas, metaphors and images of their exchanges. By switching languages they had brought me into the conversation. D'Ors' Castilian was rich and clear; not so Pahissa's, which was weak and well-larded with many Catalan idioms and expressions. Pleased with my renewed interest and attention, they increased their use of Castilian as we strolled and talked. Some two hours passed quickly; it was a pleasure to hear D'Ors talk. He would turn to me and comment in Spanish about the historic Gothic section we were crossing, describing the origin of buildings and monuments, telling their history as if he were reciting epic poems. All of it interspersed with bits of his fine humor which Pahissa and I enjoyed immensely.

As we approached the Plaza Real, I suggested that we walk a bit farther to the Rambla de Santa Mónica and allow me to invite them to some dry sherry and smoked ham at the good tavern, Casa Juan. We took a booth on the second floor. As soon as we ordered, D'Ors reach into a pocket and produced a copy of his recently published work, *La Bien Plantada*. Right then and there he autographed it for me: "To the wizard Segovia." It is one of the few and most prized books of my library saved from Civil War destruction. I have it thanks to the kindness of people I did not even know but who still risked a lot to rescue some of my books and paintings from the men who had taken over my Barcelona home.

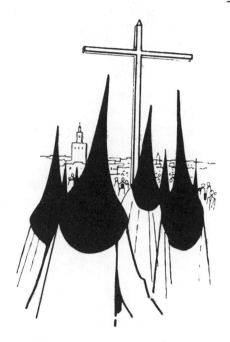

22

AFTER MY FAREWELL RECITAL at the Palau, my honorary guardian, Dr. Quiroga, returned the money I had been entrusting to him for safekeeping. I was pleasantly surprised at the amount that had accrued.

My first thought was to run to Seville and try to resume my courtship of Maria de Montis. I was sure that my Barcelona successes would be reason enough for her to forget her obstinacy and seriously consider marrying me. There was no need for her to wish I would get "a decent job," nor for us to wait for her coming of age so I could live an idle life at the expense of her forthcoming inheritance. I had no intentions of disregarding the warning of Martial, the Latin poet: "He who marries a rich woman becomes the wife of his wife." My hopes of being able to support a home were stronger than ever.

I boarded a train for Seville, and on arrival, took a room

in a pension on the street of . . . Let me explain that Seville's city fathers had changed some street names and, in order to avoid confusion, made it mandatory for the former name to appear on the slate under the new one. The roguish alderman in charge of enforcing the directive had decided to have a little fun playing word games, and so the street where my pension was located had been baptized: "Street of King Alfonso the Wise, formerly The Donkey."

The first person I looked up next morning was Miguel del Pino, the painter. I knew he had become a daily visitor to the Montis home after he painted Maria's portrait. Before calling on her, I wanted to find out if her feelings for me were still the same deep, permanent affection I expected; if her mother, brother and sister Lucita were still as friendly towards me as they had been before my departure from Seville . . .

Miguel seemed to hem and haw until he remembered it was Holy Week. Why didn't we go and wait at Sierpes Street, he suggested. Maria would be passing by with her duenna on the way to the Plaza San Fernando and the family box at the grandstand to watch the afternoon procession. We went to a strategically located café, took a table near the door, and waited.

Seville was celebrating its famous Holy Week, a festival as pagan as it is religious. The processions are an awe-inspiring display of beauty and fervor. Religious images of Montañés and other great Renaissance sculptors are paraded through the streets, mounted on floats which are veritable moving altars, escorted by the hooded members of religious fraternities. The parade stops at certain street corners to listen ecstatically to a *saeta* sung by the passionate voice of a devout Sevillian, man or woman, to his or her favorite passing image of the Virgin or Her Son. The pageantry unfolds like a series of palpitating scenes depicting the art and grace which feeds the very soul of Sevillian life. Better words than mine have described that moving festival.

Waiting for Maria to pass by, Miguel and I remembered Juanito Lafita, a mutual friend who knew aristocrats and beggars, bullfighters and venerable priests, society debutantes and sassy town belles alike; in fact, all of Seville was Juanito's friend. He used to tell a story about a ragged drunkard who

Segovia with Miguel del Pino in Seville, 1913.
Drawing by Bobri after a sketch by Miguel del Pino.

had declared himself in favor of Communism, his one hope of redemption from work, he said—as if the bottle hadn't already done the job. One day, during Holy Week, the bum was watching a procession, with its convoy of cathedral canons, priests and laity, singing hymns in Latin. Suddenly, seized by his antireligious rage, the drunk burst out shouting: "Death to the Latin race!"

There we were, Miguel del Pino and I, reminiscing in the café while we kept a watchful eye. Suddenly, Miguel exclaimed: "Here she comes!"

Seldom in my life have I been so devastatingly shocked. My heart seemed to stop as if silenced by a blow, while tears rose to my eyes. I dug my fingers on Miguel's arm as I bit the words:

"Why didn't you tell me!"

Calm, compassionate Miguel, whispered back; "If I had taken you to see her, you wouldn't have been able to conceal your surprise, and then her pain would have been all the worse. Every time she read the reviews of your concerts in Seville's newspapers, she would run to look at herself in the mirror and start crying. I thought I would spare her this one blow and let you see her alone."

In the two years since I had seen her, Maria's figure had been pathetically deformed. Her bust with its soft curves was still the same; so was her face with her charming, impish features. Her small head, now framed by the lace mantilla cascading from her high comb, was held gracefully on her slender neck. But her hips had swollen to monstrous proportions, and a similar swelling of her legs was obvious from her slow, stumbling, painful gait.

Fortunately, she did not see me. At that moment I felt a desperate tenderness towards her. But if young love enters first through the eyes, it also flees through them. I confess I lacked the selflessness to disregard the terrible change in her and accept her as she was now.

That very night, with censurable haste, I ran away to Madrid.

Through Ramírez the luthier, my friend Gaspar Cassadó,

the cellist, learned that I was in Madrid. He came to see me immediately to give me this news: Ernesto de Quesada had founded Conciertos Daniel, the first and only concert management firm I believe Madrid had then. Gaspar introduced me to the owner, general manager, clerk, and office boy, all in one person: Quesada himself. The moment we uttered the word "guitar," he stopped listening.

"I don't know a thing about that instrument, and there is nothing I can do for you," he told me.

His tone was so categorical, his gesture so final, that I turned on my heel and walked out the door. Poor Gaspar stayed behind, trying to clear the name of the guitar and its interpreters, but it was no use. He lacked the authority and even the words; at times of stress Gaspar would stutter and be unable to string five or six words together. The only thing he got out of the "impresario"—that's what the sign on Quesada's desk said—was a hasty farewell. He was too busy. He was not interested, etc. etc.

And so my mouth dropped two days later when he came into my room at the pension, followed by Gaspar. After hearing about the number of successful concerts I had given in Barcelona, Quesada had let my friend persuade him to organize a trial concert for me in Madrid, at his own expense. It would cost me nothing, but neither was I to receive a fee. A sort of public audition, in fact, since it was agreed that the recital I had given years back at the *Ateneo* didn't count. I had to start anew in the capital. By way of apology for his awful reception to me in his office, he had come personally to my pension to make the offer and discuss the date, place, and program.

I was happy with his choice of place: the ballroom of the Ritz Hotel. It was not disproportionately large, it certainly attracted a select audience, and the rental fee would not be too high—although this last consideration was not of my concern in this case. Depending on the hotel's schedule, the date could be within fifteen to twenty days. All points agreed, Ernesto de Quesada left my room.

Once again Gaspar had been alert to a development that would help further my career. What a friend, I thought, as I embraced him.

23

It was at that time that I met Clarita L. She was already a mature woman, but if her figure showed her age, she still retained much of her youthful beauty in her animated face and smiling eyes, her vivacious voice and delightful, open manner.

For some decades she had maintained an intimate relationship with the Duke of X. Not entirely without reason, the dowager duchess had fiercely opposed her son's possible marriage to the charming girl. At first, Clarita wisely advised the duke to accept his mother's prohibition, but after a few years of a quiet affair, she demanded that he marry her in secret. The duke agreed to a private ceremony and so, while respecting his mother's wishes on the surface, he in fact legalized his long liaison with his faithful lady friend.

Clarita and I met at the time when she was patiently and

with all delicacy waiting for the already very old dowager duchess to pass on so she herself could at last enjoy the rank, comforts, and fortune that went with her husband's title. Actually, the situation was known to the duke's relatives and friends and, I venture to say, even to his mother, but if the marriage was an open secret, the old duchess would not relent and acknowledge it. Clarita and the duke had shared their youth and now were growing old together.

She was very fond of music, particularly the opera, and when she heard me play, she became an admirer of the guitar. She alerted her many friends and acquaintances to my forthcoming recital at the Ritz; she wanted the most distinguished audience she could muster for the affair—although I think she would have settled for almost any audience, so long as it was a large one. Clarita did more than that in my behalf.

Wise in the ways of the world that was Madrid, she had her Tristan intercede with the duke of Santo Mauro to have the queen of Spain, Victoria Eugenia, grant me the honor of an invitation to play before her. Clarita thought that was an indispensable step in my career; it was her innocent belief that I was the magician who could transform the instrument played in taverns and heard at drunken parties into the classical guitar accepted in concert halls by people *"comme il faut."*

In the minds of followers of old monarchist traditions, the height of prestige for a musician—and an infallible step towards launching an artistic career—was to be received and heard by Their Majesties. That the king and queen were or were not qualified to pass on the merits of the artist was of little account. There were still vestiges of the time when musicians, poets, painters, and sculptors were mere servants or artisans at the service and caprices of kings, princes, and other potentates. Today royal favor has been replaced by the loyalty of thousands who sponsor artists by attending their concerts, purchasing their paintings and sculptures, and buying their books. In many cases, however, the artist, liberated from royal servitude, has fallen prey to the well-organized tyranny of agents, impresarios, art dealers, and publishers. I belong to the small fortunate group that found good friends and genuine experts among the commercial agents who managed their careers.

Conciertos Daniel made arrangements for my Madrid recital counting more on word of mouth and personal efforts than on publicity—although some press clippings did reach me advertising the event.

My friends were responsible for filling over two hundred seats to my concert at the Ritz ballroom, mostly with their friends and acquaintances. There was also the spontaneous attendance of a fair-sized group who no doubt were alerted by the few announcements which appeared in the press.

Mr. Quesada, the impresario, was tone deaf—a condition he took care to conceal. However, he had a fine sense of smell when it came to profits. He singled out those who applauded most enthusiastically at my recital and made his prediction. Next day, my favorable press reviews confirmed his impression as to my future and he immediaely attempted to sign me up for a multi-year exclusive contract. I did not sign it. It wasn't necessary. Up to the time when he retired from the field, in 1956, we were freely associated under a loose working agreement: over forty years of friendship and collaboration.

Clarita's royal plan succeeded, too! An engraved message from the palace, received at my modest pension Marlasca, informed me that I had been granted the honor of playing in the august presence of Her Majesty the Queen. I ran down and jumped on a streetcar to Clarita's house, to thank her and her Tristan and show them the royal summons. She pointed to the duke and he pointed to her, each naming the other as the logical recipient of my gratitude. Their young niece, who was present, laughed at that sort of ping-pong game.

"All right, dear friends," I said. "Clarita suggested the idea, you, Your Grace, put it into effect, and I am the beneficiary. There is still the person who made the request directly to Her Majesty. I shall express my gratitude to all by not letting anyone down: I shall play as never before, for the queen."

"I think she'd like very much to hear you play an aria from some opera," Tristan told me.

"Oh, my God," I exclaimed, "I've nothing like that in my repertoire!"

But I had a bigger problem to solve. Court etiquette called

for me to wear white tie and tails, and I had no formal clothes. So far, I had played all my concerts—including afternoon ones!—in a dinner jacket lent to me by a much taller, hefty friend; the thing billowed about me as if I were performing in a gale. It was actually the suit I had borrowed for my *Ateneo* concert years back, which the friend was kind enough to let me keep. By then, I hated it.

Of course I was terribly worried, as I told my friends at the café *Gato Negro* one afternoon. A newcomer to our group spoke up.

"You're a young artist, aren't you? We're about the same height and size. . . . Would you like to try on my dress suit?"

I was taken by his nice manners and kind gesture. He did not wait for an answer. He introduced himself:

"I am Alberto Romea, an actor, not as great as Don Julián. I play less glamorous roles, whatever playwrights and producers cast me in. I am also a guitar aficionado, but there, too, I haven't made the marquee lights. Just a dilettante. But I do have a tail coat and I heard you at the *Ateneo* and recently at the Ritz. I'd like to help you."

We left the café together and, next day, he himself brought the dress suit to my pension, together with the proper shirt and white tie, knowing I was likely to be out of those, too.

Unfortunately, we did not have a chance to pursue that budding friendship. There were my frequent absences from Madrid at first and my trips abroad. After sixteen years in America, I returned to Spain and looked him up. We had a few warm, friendly encounters, and then good old Romea died.

Maestro Emilio Serrano came to fetch and take me to the Royal Palace. Apparently, he was in charge of instructing visiting artists in the requisites of protocol in the presence of Her Majesty: bow, speak only when you are spoken to, confine yourself to answering questions, withdraw backward, bow again, etc.

We arrived at the palace, went through a summary inspection—evidently gate authorities had been informed—and proceded up the stairs to the floor above. There a very old, hunchbacked and wrinkled lady-in-waiting signaled us to stop and wait. We were in an anteroom. She disappeared, and as she opened and closed the door behind her, we could hear laughter and chatter in the next room.

I noticed a portrait of Queen Maria Luisa, wife of Charles IV. I pointed it to Maestro Serrano and softly remarked about the possible republican sentiments of the painter: he seemed to have expressed his political thoughts by emphasizing every ugly feature in the royal lady's face.

Serrano turned livid and reduced me to silence, warning me that if I said one more word, he would cancel the royal audience. Dumbfounded, I obeyed.

The tenor, Tito Schipa, arrived and joined us in a few moments. He was one of the highest paid singers in the world then. With him was Maestro Saco del Valle, the pianist who was to accompany him.

I was not happy about having to share the queen's attention with such a famous artist. My purpose—or more accurately, Clarita's—would be defeated. The queen would be delighted by Schipa's operatic arias and end up with nothing but ennui, if not disdain, for my guitar. . . . I was so distressed I was tempted to resume, in louder terms, my commentaries about the possible antimonarchist sentiments of Maria Luisa's portrait painter, so Maestro Serrano would carry out his threat and eliminate me.

Just then the same lady-in-waiting reappeared and escorted the four of us into the next room.

I was dazzled by Queen Victoria's beauty, by her imperial stance and her distinction. With a gesture which was both cool and amiable, she greeted us and thanked us for coming. Her Spanish, though fluent, still bore traces of a delightful British accent.

I could not help remember an amusing story Clarita had told me about the queen's first visit to Seville, in the days when she still did not fully understand Spanish, let alone the typical expressions of the Andalusian Spaniard in which Sevillians excel. Returning to the royal residence after a short stroll through the central city streets, the queen remarked, quite moved, "It is so charming of the Sevillians to remember my mother when they see me. . . ." She was not acquainted with the Andalusians' typical street compliment to a beautiful woman: "God bless the mother who produced that face!"

It was an expression of admiration and esteem without the slightest intention of disrespect, of course. I thought of it myself now, in front of her.

She first greeted Schipa and told him how much she enjoyed his performances at the Teatro Real, a gracious compliment which Schipa acknowledged awkwardly, stammering: *"Grazie, Signora, grazie!"* while he bowed so low that his body formed a right angle with his stiff legs.

Then the queen turned to me. "Where are you from, young man?" she asked.

Just to be different from the rattled Schipa, I threw caution and protocol to the wind and answered, "From a region of Spain where Your Majesty is greatly admired."

She smiled, but kept her eyes on me, waiting for my answer.

I threw more caution away. "Of course, it is not easy to say which region of Spain admires Your Majesty the most," and, starting to bow, not quite as low as Schipa, I added, "I am Andalusian, milady! From Linares."

Maestro Saco del Valle, the pianist, suggested that I open the recital, thus giving Tito Schipa the place of honor in the program. I found it quite natural. Schipa was an internationally renowned tenor, and I was a beginning artist with hardly a reputation in Spain itself; he had been invited to the Royal Palace after countless successes in the most important theaters of Europe, and I was there only on the recommendation of a high court official; his repertory abounded in outstanding operas, and mine in music that probably was not known to that illustrious audience. . . .

Following the queen's smiling indication, I took my guitar and played a short program of pieces which I thought would please my royal listener and her small retinue. At the end, she came toward me, smiling warmly. "Young man, you play like . . . like . . ." She was searching for the words which could best express her pleasure. I waited and at last she found them: ". . . Like a music box!"

137

I bowed, smiling to myself, but nevertheless aware of her delicate compliment.

"I have yet to reach that point of perfection, Your Majesty," I said.

"How modest!" she exclaimed.

I wanted to show Schipa the courtesy of remaining to hear him, but that chicken-hearted Maestro Serrano, no doubt fearing I might again utter the word "republic" in the royal presence, gave me a sign indicating that my audience was concluded and I should follow him. I withdrew backward to the door of the chamber and, following court etiquette, made my final bow before my master of ceremonies and left the room. Outside, the same lady-in-waiting who had received us placed a small package in my hand, a gift from Her Majesty.

Serrano and I parted out in the street, I to hail a carriage —I don't think there were taxis yet in Madrid. I gave the witty, talkative coachman an address on Lista Street, the residence of the count and countess of Casa Miranda.

I had met the three members of that family through Clarita. Shortly after my arrival in Madrid from Seville, I went to call on Clarita and there was Helena Gilinska, the adopted niece of the count and countess. She was a beautiful blond young Polish girl, with smiling sky-blue eyes which could suddenly become melancholy or dreamy, depending on whether she was thinking of the past or anticipating the future. She spoke Spanish well, although she often charmingly confused certain idiomatic expressions.

It did not take us long to become friends. Clarita said that Helena sang quite well, particularly the works of Italian classics and German romantics. I so wanted to hear her, that the girl finally sent for her pianist. I, in turn, sent for my guitar, and so she sang for me and I played for her. The artistic exchange developed into a mutual attraction which in a few weeks of frequent visits and encounters was to grow into a deep affection. It was then that the sad effects of my Sevillian experience with my poor Maria de Montis began to fade.

The day after we first met at Clarita's, Helena took me to her home and introduced me to her aunt and uncle. Rosita, countess of Casa Miranda, was the daughter or a former Spanish ambassador to France. She married Frede de la Cárcel, a distinguished man and sensitive art lover who was especially fond of music. The war—it was 1917—had sent them back to Spain and peace after they closed their home in Paris. He had countless stories to tell me about his friendship with Kreisler, Godowsky, Mischa Elman and other musical celebrities of the time. He also knew and admired José Iturbi, for whom he predicted a brilliant future. He told me how the young Valencian pianist would swear like a trooper when his fingers wouldn't respond to his commands on the keyboard.

The Casa Mirandas had welcomed me warmly into their home, and so I went directly to them from the Royal Palace. They were anxious to hear all about my recital before the queen. Helena insisted that I describe the event with full details. I complied, scene by scene; the fright I unwittingly gave my poor court mentor with my reference to the "republican" portrait painter; my impression of the queen's cool beauty, regal bearing and measured cordiality, her amusing search for the right compliment to me, and the ingenious—and mischievous—solution to which we both arrived at the end with our "music box." We opened the little package I had received. It was a gold tiepin with the initials RV (Victoria Regina) in diamond chips, beneath a tiny version of the royal crown in semiprecious red stones—an attractive gift to be prized as a souvenir rather than for its intrinsic value. Helena liked it very much, and the count and countess complimented it courteously.

At the end, when Helena said good-bye to me at the door, I gave her the little pin. At first she resisted accepting it, but I insisted. At last she took it, rewarding me with a kiss that set my whole being on fire.

Years later, Tito Schipa and I met on an ocean liner that was taking us from Genoa to New York. There was a benefit performance for the Seamen's Fund on board. Schipa sang that night—his voice already less bell-like than when he had sung for the queen. He wore on his lapel a pin similar to mine, but—larger, finer, encrusted with substantial, brilliant diamonds and rubies. What a difference! Court protocol had certainly made a distinction between our artistic reputations. I reminded Schipa of the occasion.

"They didn't give you anything, did they?" he asked, smiling.

"Nothing," I answered.

Quesada, my new impresario, wanted to test provincial concert audiences and suggested that I accept a limited tour of Spain's most "musical" cities. He was well aware that some of the reigning music societies had crossed my name off their list of performing artists, more against the guitar than against me, in accord with the joint influence of Maestro Arbós and Fernández Bordas—the last one director of the Madrid Conservatory. Both were violinists, although neither retained any vestige of performing virtuosity. Señor Quesada was counting on the attendance of spontaneous public to my concerts, not on the members and followers of those music societies.

One had to admire Quesada for risking his investment. The expenses of my tour were not minor. There was the renting of halls and theaters, publicity expenditures, the fee and travel expenses of the "advance man" who would be traveling with me, and my own living to be made, however modest. I was very grateful to him.

We began the tour, young del Rio and I—he was Quesada's most trusted and hardworking employee. Unless I am mistaken, our first stop was the city of Bilbao, in the Basque country.

The result of the first concert was most promising, and a jubilant del Rio wired the details to his boss. Quesada answered back with congratulations.

Young del Rio was a friendly and amusing traveling companion. He refused to allow his short stature to inhibit him. In fact, he would often make jokes about it. It would fill this book if I were to tell of our adventures and the people we met during that tour. There is one incident, however, which I would like to recall. It took place in the Galician city of Vigo, in northwestern Spain.

I lost my wallet in Vigo—or some expert pickpocket stole it from me. However I did lose it, the wallet contained the proceeds of my concerts—little enough, but still all the cash I had.

I was distressed, angry, even enraged. I could not eat, drink, or sleep. How could I, when I was unable to pay my bill at the pension, buy a railroad ticket, or even tip the porter who would carry my things to the station. Being the "advance man" in the tour, del Rio had already left for the next stop; his job was to precede me by a few days and prepare the following concert in our schedule. I just didn't have the heart to inform him of my predicament and risk worrying him and interfering with all the chores and details he had to take care of prior to my arrival. I had no friends in Vigo, no possibility of playing there again. The situation was driving me to distraction.

Turning the problem over and over in my mind, I decided to spend what change I had left in my pocket to wire an old friend in Madrid, the consul general of a Spanish-American republic. He knew me well enough to realize I wasn't just "touching" him for a handout. I explained the situation briefly in the telegram and begged him to wire me five hundred *pesetas.*

A week went by and I received no answer. I still remember my anguish at being so hopelessly stranded. Not so hopelessly, after all. Del Rio, who was waiting for me in Burgos, became worried at my long delay and telephoned me in Vigo. I had no alternative but to tell him what had happened. He wired his boss in Madrid and solved the problem.

Now comes the best part of the story. I was bitter and indignant at the deaf ear that my consular friend in Madrid had paid to my urgent telegram. The resentment turned to glee when I hit upon what I thought would be a marvelous way to reproach him for his oblivion to my distress.

From my share of the proceeds of the next three or four concerts after Burgos, I set aside five hundred *pesetas,* the amount I had asked him for and never received. As if I were "paying back" the nonexistent loan, I sent him a postal money order together with a sarcastic note thanking him for the speed with which he had gone to my rescue when I was stranded in Vigo.

His reaction was more baffling than his silence to my S.O.S. He kept the money and never acknowledged having heard from me by telegram or letter. I never heard from him again. I thought that protesting or trying to get back my money would only duplicate my idiocy in sending it in the first place.

Years later, the man was serving his country again as consul general in a Spanish-American city where I was scheduled to play a well-publicized concert. He tried to get in touch with me by phone. My manager, Señor Quesada, happened to be with me when the call came. I asked Quesada to answer it with this message: "Andrés Segovia would appreciate the belated courtesy of knowing whether you received repayment of the money you so quickly and generously sent him when he wired you from Vigo, Mr. Consul."

He did not even answer. He hung up without a word, which, of course, revived my indignation. I left the city without ever speaking with him.

Noblesse oblige, however: in time, he did come through with his acknowledgment. In 1938 he was his country's ambassador to Brazil. There, in Rio de Janeiro, he heard of the birth of my daughter Beatriz in Montevideo. Through diplomatic channels, he sent the child a solid gold cross encrusted with diamonds, with its heavy gold chain and this note: "Beatriz, wear this well when you grow up and let it remind you of someone who had the misfortune of displeasing your father and losing his friendship."

The gift was worth several times the amount that had caused the rift between us. But the timely and delicate gesture was priceless.

Needless to say, I wrote to him immediately offering to forget the whole unpleasant incident and resume our old friendship. He never got to read my letter. Shortly after takeoff, a commercial plane he had boarded in Rio collided in midair with a private craft and crashed down into the bay. His had been an uneventful life; he was a cultured man, a moderately talented writer, and a knowledgeable art and music lover. His name has almost been forgotten, but it is not up to me to mention it, especially after the incidents I have narrated above.

24

TEN DAYS after the outbreak of the Spanish Civil War, on July 28, 1938, to be exact, I left Spain to return only sixteen years later. I soon heard that my home in Barcelona had been sacked. Everything that the vandals did not consider of commercial value was destroyed. I lost manuscripts of famous Spanish and foreign composers, my correspondence with illustrious friends, and works of art and books which had been inscribed to me by the authors.

According to other tenants in the house, the ignorant looters sold valuable objects and first editions for a pittance. Whatever they could not sell they burned for fuel. Poor people! If the spiritual light of those treasures could not illuminate their minds, at least the bonfires they made with them warmed their bodies. So my library served a practical purpose to the end.

A multitude of treasured souvenirs of my trips to the Far East, Peru, Mexico, and other countries—Oriental silks and tapestries, wrought silver, tableware, etc.—wound up in public markets and changed hands in back-street transactions. It was not uncommon for an innocent buyer of such property to be visited by shady individuals posing as members of some revolutionary group or political committee who, under the guise of legality would intimidate the poor soul and confiscate his purchase. That type of rabble thrives in any war and demeans any flag.

Fourteen times in my life I've had to set up a home anew; three before the Spanish Civil War and eleven others afterwards. And I don't mean local moves from one quarter to another in a given city. I mean in Geneva, Barcelona, Montevideo, New York, Madrid . . . and, finally, in a rural homestead in the province of Granada, surrounded by olive trees, tall pines and willows, with a backdrop of high mountains and open skies, and a sweeping view of the sea in the distance.

Thus I lost much of my notes and records and must now rely heavily on my memory, which is still excellent for music, pretty good for people, events and places, and . . . terrible for dates, as ever. Still, I am well ahead of a friend of mine who used to complain bitterly about his consistently poor memory, a failure he attributed to three irritating facts: "First," he would say, "I just can't remember names and faces; second, I can't retain what I read; and third . . . What is the third one? Oh, my God, I forgot already!"

A friend, Ramón Goy del Silva, took me to the studio of Madame Shilnerowa, a Czechoslovakian painter who had arrived in Madrid some months before. She was spending long hours at the Prado Museum, tirelessly copying the works of Velázquez. Her purpose was to develop a more flexible brush and greater perception for line and color—although, she knew well she could not copy the genius that had gone into those paintings.

No longer in the prime of youth, and shortchanged by nature in beauty and feminine grace, Shilnerowa nevertheless was extremely generous and possessed a warm, vivid personality. She was so appealing that critics who before meeting her had censured her work severely, would change their criticism to friendly advice once they knew her personally. I saw the change in "Juan de Encina," Madrid's leading art critic at that time. I also saw it in Vegue, the writer-lecturer whose nickname was "Odol" because his twisted neck resembled the curved bottle of the famous mouthwash. Vegue's lectures and conferences earned him the not always justifiable derision of Madrid's aggressive artists.

Shilnerowa was candid and good-natured about her poor luck with the critics. Quite openly she would tell everyone about a terror of a demanding Prague critic who, at the request of one of her influential patrons, had finally consented to visit her studio. He looked at her paintings one by one, in total silence. No comment, no praise, no criticism. Then, on his way out the door, he saw a blank canvas on the easel, awaiting the first strokes. Smiling, but with a bitter undertone, Shilnerowa would finish the story: The man pointed to the blank canvas and advised her, "My dear, don't touch it any more!"

Shilnerowa shared her home and studio with a Russian student to whom she was teaching drawing, Mademoiselle Malinowska. This strange girl was crowned with a mass of ash-blonde hair worn in wild disarray. Her enormous blue eyes reflected her variable moods and expressions. At times, her small face would look attractive and composed; the next second her features became ugly and somehow out of kilter.

Malinowska's unpredictable changes were surprising and at times amusing. She was a living example of the contradictory and impetuous traits attributed to the Slavs. That, together with her normal feminine changeability, was something to behold. I, who visited her often, couldn't help laugh at her disparate moods and behavior.

The Spanish housemaids had taught both foreign ladies many foul words and expressions picked up in the slums of Madrid. Shilnerowa was careful not to repeat them, but young Malinowska thought nothing of blurting them out in front of visitors, coloring her chatter with them, to the amusement and laughter of all present. At that, she would hide her face, exclaiming: "Oh, how shameful of me to be so shameless!"

In time, Madame Shilnerowa made good friends among the city's writers, musicians and painters. Her salons, held every two weeks, were attended by the most select intellectuals of Madrid. At the first such gathering I attended I saw the Zubiaurre brothers, both successful painters, particularly Valentín; Baroja, the painter, brother of the writer, Pio Baroja; the picturesque writer, Jacinto Grau and his editor-apologist, Ricardo Baeza; "Sister" Enrique Diez-Canedo, whose high-pitched voice and sweet lilt had earned him his "nun" title— none of which detracted from his solid reputation as one of the best translators of Italian, French and English poetry into Spanish. He was a man of immense cultural resources who could devise the most faithful and accurate equivalents for incredibly remote images in the original's language.

That first day at Shilnerowa's I met two illustrious figures of those days whose friendship I enjoyed until they passed away: poet and playwright, Eduardo Marquina, and the painter-novelist Santiago Rusiñol. Marquina's profitable stage successes caused him the envy of colleagues and critics. He had a tendency for using actors as heralds, with exalted lines like "Spain Heroic!" but still, his collection of poems, *Elegies*, established him as one of the ranking poets of his time.

Also present that afternoon were the great Spanish writer, José Ortega y Gasset, who was joined there later by his brother Eduardo. I had already crossed swords with Don José, when I dared contradict him in certain points of his essay, *Musicalia*. Since then he had written me out of the human race. Now he was ignoring me completely, to the extent of speaking to mutual friends I was talking with, as if I weren't there at all. Thinking we had not yet met, Madame Shilnerowa attempted to introduce us. I stopped her gently in time and veered towards the perpetually pleasant Santiago Rusiñol.

Everyone loved and admired Don Santiago for many reasons beside his knowledge and understanding of all fields of literature and art. He had a kind and cheerful disposition; he was always simpatico and approachable. There were countless

146

stories about his bohemian life—safely backed by a good income. He paid no attention to the inevitable envy that his talent aroused; he was much too good a person to mind.

I sat next to him and told him how years back, as a boy, I had watched him from a distance as he painted in the gardens of the Generalife, absorbed in his work, oblivious to all activity surrounding him. Not even the self-styled king of the gypsies, *Chorro-Humo* (Fuming Jet!), was able to distract him, as he approached with catlike caution, hand extended, to ask for a handout. Barely taking his eyes from his work, Don Santiago put his hand in his pocket, produced a few coins, and gave them to "His Majesty," who scurried away in quest of a more lucrative prey among an approaching group of tourists.

Once, together with Ramón Casas—another fine painter— Santiago Rusiñol made a memorable tour of Catalonian *pueblos*. Some claimed that the journey had been made by donkey, others that a cart had been used. When asked to clarify the means of transportation, Santiago would say, "Both versions are correct. The donkey pulled the cart."

The two painter-friends would stop in a *pueblo*, go to the public market, spread a black cloth on the pavement, and place on it little mounds of five-*peseta* coins, the beautiful silver *duros* of those days. Then they would hawk their wares: "*Duros* for eighteen *reales!*" The *duro* was worth TWENTY *reales*— as a quarter is worth twenty-five cents!

It was a trick to test the countryfolk. Bargain hunters would stop, pick up a *duro*, weigh it in their hands, bite into it, try to bend it, and . . . finally drop it back on the cloth and walk away, suspicion and disappointment in their eyes. Not one of them took up the pranksters' challenge! Real, legitimate *duros* fresh from the teller's window at the local bank!

Santiago Rusiñol . . . I can't help recalling a pen-portrait of him by Spanish-America's harbinger of modern Spanish poetry, Rubén Darío. Here is a free translation:

> The kindly Catalan who tamed the light,
> Gardener of ideas and the Sun . . .
> Praised be his brush, his pen, his beard and laughter,
> With all of them Rusiñol brought us joy.

147

We became friends from the start, Rusiñol and I. He attended my concerts in Barcelona and right after one of them, one night, he invited me to spend some days at his home in Sitges, "Cau Ferrat," which, by the way, is used today as a city museum of Catalonian paintings, and valuable works of wrought iron and stained glass.

One morning at the Cau Ferrat, I was practicing and going over newly received guitar transcriptions, when a rough but prosperous Catalonian peasant from a neighboring *pueblo* came to visit Rusiñol. My host, who had been sittting next to me, signaled the man to wait until I could finish the piece I was playing. I rushed a bit to the end so they could talk, and the moment I played the last bar, the peasant burst out in dead earnest, in typical idioms of the Catalonian countryfolk:

"My God, how this kid plays! It's a shame he is not blind. The money he could make playing in the streets!"

Another friend who earned our admiration and affection at Shilnerowa's salons was the delicious Margot Calleja. She was just over twenty and, as Fedcrico García Lorca used to say, she had *duende*, "it," that ineffable charm. Góngora could have said his famous lines to her:

Muchos siglos de hermosura	Many centuries of beauty
en pocos años de edad.	condensed in a few years.

Margot was not the proverbial "beauty"—vain, presumptuous, provocative. On the contrary. She seemed to ignore her charms and always acted with exquisite discretion, just cheerful enough, with her fine, open smile, her lithe figure and subtly elegant clothes. I lost contact with her when I went to tour abroad, but I learned of her marriage to a German diplomat. Later on there was some tragic news I was never able to verify: the Nazis had discovered that her husband's Aryan background was in doubt, and he was sentenced to suffer the atrocities of a concentration camp. I haven't yet found a relative or friend of theirs who could deny or confirm that report.

25

Max Nordau

IT WAS ALSO AT Shilnerowa's studio that I met the then famous essayist, Max Nordau. I had already read his controversial works, *Degeneration* and *The Conventional Lies of Our Civilization*. In the first one he launches a severe attack against genuine artistic and intellectual values of his time. Pity, I thought, that Nordau had not been endowed with Jahweh's gift of prophecy—later usurped by Nostradamus. I am sure he would have found a lot more deserving targets for his attacks in the demolishers of art, poetry, and moral thought of this turbulent era. As for the second book, he said great world truth in it; but there, too, he did so in extremely harsh, sarcastic terms.

Nordau was a short man, but he stood out in a crowd because of his enormous double chin—a goiter which deformed his neck and forced him to wear outsize collars, like a clown.

He would flare up into a rage for the most innocuous reason, perhaps because of some irritation caused by his deformity. He spoke French well and very rapidly. We marveled at the clarity, precision, and diversity of all his ideas.

Nordau, who was born in Budapest, had fled Paris when France and the Central European powers tangled up and went to war. He didn't feel safe until he reached Spain. He lived with his wife and two daughters on a narrow street of the Plaza de Oriente, in the middle of metropolitan Madrid. Madame Nordau was a tall, dry, thin, lethargic woman of few words. Lily, their eldest, was a lanky and awkward overgrown girl with the voice of a chirping bird and a brain to match. She sat squirming, crossing and uncrossing her legs and arms at tempo with her words, with the desperate restlessness of an old maid; a copy of her mother—a defective one, to boot.

Maxa, the younger daughter, was the reverse: an improved version of her father. She was short and plump. No thought or feeling seemed to leave a trace in her smooth, wide forehead. There was always a smile in her sensuous, full lips, echoed by her equally smiling eyes. The only feature that disrupted her pleasant expression was a large hook nose. Like her father, she was intelligent and spoke fast and with precision. She was soon speaking as fluently in Spanish as she did in French.

Maxa was an accomplished art student and was looking for a good art teacher in Madrid. That is what had brought them to Shernilowa's studio the afternoon we met. While the girl toured the studio and looked at paintings, the rest of us sat around her father. Nordeau greeted me warmly and surprised me by saying he had attended my second recital at the *Ateneo.*

"Out of curiosity," he explained. "I thought there was going to be flamenco singing, dancing, tapping, with corresponding olés and sherry—all to the music of Bach, Mozart and Haydn you were scheduled to play on the guitar. At the respectable *Ateneo!* The whole thing intrigued me so I just had to go. However, what you played and *how* you played impressed me very much."

After I thanked him, he continued. "Watching you play, I thought how well those poor French soldiers could use your nimble fingers to scratch themselves in those miserable trenches."

We laughed at that curious bit of black humor, and Goy de Silva, always touchy and humorless, but nevertheless an admiring friend, whispered in my ear, "You can't feel flattered at that crazy application he's proposing for your wonderful technique."

I shrugged my shoulders, gave him a placating sign, and went back to listening to the philosopher.

Maxa joined our group. Pointing to me, her father told her, "This is the young guitarist we heard last year at the *Ateneo*, remember?"

"That's right!" she exclaimed. "Of course I remember now. No wonder I thought I had seen you before."

Quietly and discreetly, without offense to Shilnerowa's paintings which she had just seen, she told us her problem: she really wanted to study with a *Spanish* painter. Goy de Silva mentioned the name of a much-admired painter he befriended, José María López Mezquita. The moment Nordau heard the name, he went right on to describe all that Mezquita's works had suggested when he saw them either at the Museum of Modern Art or in reproductions; his vigorous style, the accurate likeness of his portraits, the spiritual quality he imparted to his work . . .

At that time, Mezquita was about to finish my portrait, so I offered to introduce Maxa to him. I knew the painter was not acquainted with the philosopher or his works. Goy de Silva and I tried hard to persuade him to take on Maxa as a student—although we both knew why the decision wouldn't be up to him. Mezquita had to consult a capricious and authoritarian Mexican lady who, though married into Madrid's aristocracy, had a tight hold on the painter's heartstrings.

After making thorough inquiries into the Nordaus' background and glancing at Maxa's nose, the lady granted Mezquita permission to give the girl a two-hour daily lesson.

I used to visit the Nordaus frequently. Maxa would gather her group of friends and receive us in her room, the largest in the apartment. Occasionally her father would join rather than dampen our fun. He would fall right in step with our youthful mood and delight us with amusing and instructive anecdotes. Since they often had to be translated into Spanish for those who did not understand French, the impression remained more indelible in our minds.

We always met Helena Adoryan at those gatherings. She was a close friend of Maxa and herself Hungarian. Like the Nordaus and for the same reason, her family, too, had taken refuge in Madrid. I got to meet them and visit them quite often. Her mother, a heavy lady who spoke only Magyar, smoked thick, long cigars. When not enveloped in a cloud of smoke, she reeked of the bitter smell of her last cigar. Her company was most disagreeable. I never met the father; he had died shortly after arriving in Madrid, leaving the family in the most difficult financial situation.

Helena was not beautiful, but she had—to use the current expression—sex appeal and plenty of it, although she never flaunted her femininity or put her reputation in jeopardy by wasting it in casual flirtations. Maxa begged us to help her by recommending her as a French, German, English, or Hungarian translator. I spoke to Clarita at once about the girl, and soon Clarita found her work, translating for important commercial firms and also giving private language lessons. I never regretted it. She was highly praised for her efficiency and her proper behavior.

But, oh, her brother! That singular creature defies description. To do him justice would require a better writing craft than mine. To begin with, he had a speech defect since birth; not only were his words unintelligible, they were also interspersed with the most unsettling little grunts. He was unable to coordinate an idea and carry it through to verbal expression. In other words, with no offense meant to him or his family, he was an idiot. And, don't anyone think me unkind. Please read on.

I couldn't believe it when Helena begged me, with the most relentless persistence, to introduce her brother to *La Gran Peña*, Madrid's most aristocratic men's club. What on earth for, was my first, anguished thought. So that he could enter the forthcoming International Billiard Tournament scheduled to take place in said club! While Helena explained all that and continued to plead with me, I threw a distressed glance in the direction of that incomplete, unfortunate young man. How could he possess the miraculous ability his sister attributed to him? I say that because by now Helena was warning me—or predicting—that he could well win the championship!

I knew no one on the club's committee, but I thought of going to the Duke of Bivona, who I knew was an influential member of the club. He was always generous and accessible. Why not go to him.

The duke was not in Madrid then, but I was received by the duchess. When I told her the purpose of my visit, she was as surprised as I had been by Helena. The duchess knew the girl and had already helped her. She had heard of her brother's drawbacks. Like me, she found it extremely hard to believe that he was capable of doing anything except vegetate and laze away in the seclusion of his home. However, if only for poor Helena, we agreed to speak to the duke and see what could be done about verifying that strange young man's reported ability. In a few days the duke telephoned me and made an appointment for us to meet him at *La Gran Peña*.

We were met at the club's door in the name of the duke and escorted into the Billiard Salon—that's what they called it. One of the contestants, a foreigner of undetermined nationality, was practicing at the main table. Taking no notice of us, he continued playing for five or six more minutes. At last he straightened up, looked at us, and without the slightest hesitation, handed me the cue. I smiled and passed the thing on to my protégé. Said protégé took it, mouth open and tongue tip peering between his lips. He rubbed chalk on the cue tip and, without much ado, hit the ivory ball with infinite tenderness and sent it careening down the felt, to kiss the others awaiting at the proper place.

For one hour, the "incomplete, unfortunate" young man performed marvels at that table without a single fault or stumble. Not once did he make an error—to the consternation and delight of all those present, including the foreign star who had preceded him. He was invited to try all sorts of combinations whose names—forgive me, I'm not an expert—I could not recall. They handed him longer cues, shorter ones, heavy ones, light ones. . . . Whatever he tried, he passed the test with flying colors, quietly and . . . elegantly!

Among the crowd watching the prodigy, I caught a glimpse of the duke's face. The moment our eyes met, we walked toward each other.

"He's incredible!" he whispered to me. "This strange creature has poured his whole inner being into this game. The balls obey him as if he hypnotized them. He's a magician!"

I had to leave Madrid for a few weeks and went to see the Adoryans as soon as I returned. Helena embraced me warmly.

The duke had thought it best that her brother decline the invitation to enter the tournament, she explained. "Maybe because of his wild look, poor dear," she added. "But the club gave him a generous consolation prize. And you know what? They call on him often to go and play for groups of aficionados, and they pay him every time! We're so grateful to you. We have some money coming in now, and . . . my brother is so happy!"

26

THE NUMBER OF RECITALS I was giving outside Madrid was increasing. It was most encouraging. Even though my earnings remained very modest, my artistic career was on the way up.

As I played with increasing success in provincial cities, various local concert societies disregarded Maestro Arbós' dictum against the "musical" guitar and added my name to their list of forthcoming attractions. The first one to break the ice for me was in the city of Gijón, and for its courage and daring I have always been grateful. Next in line, if I remember correctly, was the city of Málaga. There, however, the president of the society feared the wrath of the members if he organized for them a totally "guitaristic" program, and decided to feature me together with a renowned Russian singer of the time, Madame Lahowska. She was to be accompanied by José Maria

Franco, a pianist who had and deserved a fine reputation. Not so bad, I thought.

Señor Quesada, my enterprising agent, wanted to make one more test before tackling a more ambitious project. His plan was to present me at Madrid's large and reputable Teatro de la Comedia. If that proved successful with public and critics, he would then organize for me a tour of Uruguay, Argentina and Chile for the following fall season.

At first I was elated, but then I began to think. So far, few Madrid dailies had devoted space to me; and then only brief, favorable notices, never a detailed review or a long article. In four years I had only played as many times in the Spanish capital; twice for the general public, at the Ritz; twice for the closed membership of a private club, the *Ateneo*.

How different Barcelona had been for me, in comparison to impenetrable Madrid! At the Catalonian city I had been confident enough to give my farewell concert at the vast, prestigious Palau. Here in Madrid I was inhibited by the possibility of drawing only small audiences. It had been relatively easy to fill a small ballroom like the Ritz—but how would it be at the enormous theater of La Comedia? If only a straggling few went to hear me, it could be a serious setback for my career.

I let Quesada know my qualms. He dismissed them quickly and finally got my consent to go ahead with his plan. He would cover all the expenses, and I would get a percentage of the box office receipts.

"They'll hear about this Madrid concert in Buenos Aires, can't you see?" he told me, to allay my fears.

He was right, in the end. All my friends did their share toward a full house. Clarita L., my good friend, bought and made gifts of a good number of expensive seats. The count and countess of Casa Miranda refused my invitation; they would purchase and pay for their own tickets, thank you. Not so their niece Helena. She would not need a ticket; she wanted to be with me from the moment I left my room at the pension until I reached the little room off stage. She was determined to help steady my nerves and steel my confidence—things I needed from her more than from anyone else. I gave away two boxes and a few single seats to friends I knew could not afford the admission price.

Victory! Every seat in the house was filled. The public received me with a warmth and appreciation beyond my expectations. And the critics? They put aside their moth-eaten hostility towards the classical guitar and were surprisingly kind and receptive to the instrument's fanatical apostle: yours truly.

Quesada was beaming. He would start negotiations at once with his Buenos Aires associates.

Thank God, there was a chance for me outside Spain as well!

One morning I got to Quesada's office—Conciertos Daniel, Los Madrazo Street number 14, how could I forget it—and was stunned by the beauty, garb, and grace of a young woman sitting in the waiting room. She was accompanying a friend—as I learned later, a Mexican pianist, Carmen Rangel, who was exploring the possibility of giving a presentation concert in Madrid.

That splendorous young creature was Adelaida Portillo. I had seen her before.

"You dazzled me in Seville a couple of years ago," I told her.

"Really?" she said, with a tropical accent which recalled swaying palm trees. "And I see you still don't wear dark glasses."

"They called you 'the savage beauty' in Seville."

"I know. The one who started that looked as if he had just come out of a jungle himself. You know what I told him? 'I don't know if I am a beauty, sir, but you certainly are a savage.' "

When the two young women got ready to leave, I asked their permission to accompany them. Quesada, who was next to us, interrupted. "Andrés, please, we have to talk . . ."

"Leave it for tomorrow," I said.

I walked the young ladies to their pension, not far from Quesada's office—unfortunately for me, since we got there much too soon. However, on the way, I learned that the girl was the daughter of a colonel in the Corps of Engineers, and a

Cuban lady. Her father, at that time stationed in Madrid, was about to be transferred to Cádiz, in the south of Spain.

"Señorita . . ." I said.

"My name is Adelaida."

"Thank you. May I visit you?"

"We'll see. Perhaps you can call tomorrow, I'm expecting some friends then. We're meeting at Carmen's room. My father is very straitlaced and doesn't approve much of young visitors. Come if you like."

We arrived at her door. It wasn't easy to tear myself from her. The images of all the girls who had made my heart beat faster till then began to fade away. From that morning on, Adelaida became the sole object of my yearning.

We met frequently in the following months. At times I would invite her, her friend and her mother, to have tea at Molinero's. On occasion, she and Carmen would stroll with me through the gardens of El Retiro. Soon I began noticing Señora Portillo's displeasure. Her hostility towards me annoyed me, of course, but it also pleased me because it meant she realized that her daughter looked favorably on me as a suitor.

I was not going to send the girl an awkward letter declaring my love, least of all could I do it verbally: whenever we were alone, I got a knot in my throat and could not utter a word. Walking along, side by side, burning to tell her my feelings, I couldn't help think of that subtle Andalusian stanza:

¡Dímelo andando,	Tell me as we stroll along,
dímelo andando!	tell me as we stroll along!
Que si tu tienes miedo	You may be afraid,
yo voy temblando . . ."	but I'm trembling with love.

One morning, we looked deep into each other's eyes and . . . the tight clasp of our hands sealed our fate.

Her mother was beside herself with distress when she heard about it. "My daughter in love with a youngster who has no fortune and no career! A mere *tocaor!*" (Apparently she thought I played guitar in some tavern.) "Oh, God, don't let her! Don't let her marry *him!*" That's what she would go

158

around wailing in the house, according to our friend Carmen. And when the lady found it necessary to tell her husband, he flew into a rage audible in the surrounding blocks. Adelaida had expected it; she took it calmly and waited for the storm to blow over.

In a couple of days I received a letter which, although signed by the colonel, seemed to have been dictated by his drill sergeant. I wish I could give the reader a good laugh by reproducing it verbatim. I lost it, but I well remember the gist of it: I should harbor no illusions; his daughter was not going to marry a good-for-nothing like me. . . . He had been reliably informed that my sole aim was to get my hands on her dowry so I could hang up my guitar for good the moment we would walk out of the church. My alleged love did not exist, it was all part of a plan to this and that and the other. . . .

In my answer, I told the irate colonel that he was only offending his daughter by supposing that her beauty and her grace could not inspire genuine love in a sensitive young man. His ugly accusations and exceptionable language could not touch me. His mind was obviously closed tight against any form of human understanding, let alone of art; thus his un-called-for fury at his daughter's choice of an artist for husband. "Well, dear colonel, your daughter is already over the age of consent and no longer legally bound to follow her parents' will. Therefore, in spite of your bellicose attitude, we are getting married soon, sir!"

Adelaida, for her part, sought the help and support of her cousins, the Canga-Argüelles, who lived not far, on the Street of Alcalá. They, in turn, asked the family physician and close friend, Dr. Sandoval, to meet and speak with me. The idea was to sound me out as to my plans and feelings, my morals, habits, and above all, my economic prospects for the future. Depending on the doctor's verdict, Adelaida would be dissuaded from or seconded in her choice.

The doctor and I became fine friends at that exhaustive questioning. I had taken the precaution of carrying with me Quesada's contract for my South American tour. That convinced Dr. Sandoval. This time the artist won and the colonel lost!

159

One afternoon, the young sculptor Victorio Macho came to see me. He was already enjoying a well-deserved artistic reputation. He brought me a message from no less an illustrious figure than the patriarch of Spanish letters, Benito Pérez Galdós. The grand old man of literature wanted to hear me play, but he was almost blind by then. Would I save him the inconvenience of a trip and go to him, instead?

Would I! I was elated. Since my childhood Galdós had fired my imagination and filled my soul with feelings of love, admiration, even indignation and hatred for the vivid characters I met in his books. In my early youth I had devoured the first two series of his *Episodios Nacionales,* and his novels *Gloria, Doña Perfecta,* and others as well known. I had immersed myself in the world he had created with his immensely prolific pen.

I knew the master loved music—contrary to most Spanish writers. I had never understood, for instance, how a Valle-Inclán, himself a great stylist with a fine ear for the poetry of our language, could have been so insensitive to the poetry of music. Galdós, on the contrary, not only had that sensitive ear; he was a musician in his own right. He had played the piano and the organ and was known to admire Bach, Mozart, Beethoven . . . That alone increased my warm feelings for him.

And so, I got ready to play for him pieces of the great masters and others by Sor, Giuliani, Tárrega . . . Perhaps, I thought, this curiosity to hear me play will turn into a genuine appreciation for the new language he will discover in the guitar.

And that was exactly what happened. Towards the end of the program I played the andante of Beethoven's *Pathétique,* and Galdós hummed the melody softly from start to finish. At the end, he took my hand and raised it to his lips. I've seldom been so moved. The generous, impulsive gesture had been witnessed and enjoyed by friends of the maestro, among them sculptor Victorio Macho himself, Cristóbal Ruiz, Goy de Silva. That tribute from Pérez Galdós is one of the most priceless rewards I have received in my whole life.

Two days later, on May 25, 1918, a story about that unforgettable private recital appeared in *La Correspondencia de España* and, subsequently, in other Spanish publications.

160

27

THE SUMMER OF 1918 I spent some time in Bayona, a little town near Vigo, on one of the most attractive Galician estuaries of the Atlantic coast. I went there with a friend, Fernando Calleja, one of the directors of the well-known publishers of the same name. He was a strange and difficult young man. A deep cleft seemed to split his forehead in two. Resting on his snub nose and biting it to the bleeding point were his thick eyeglasses. His lips looked as if they had been turned inward, they were so thin. He had a permanent expression of ill humor which accurately reflected his sour character.

We took rooms in one of the typical pensions of the region. It wasn't as clean as the boardinghouses of Andalusia, where everything seems not only clean but polished. Still, my room was furnished with solid if not elegant pieces, and the bed was wide and stacked with thick mattresses, a veritable "battlefield of love."

The pension was run by a woman over forty, pleasant and still nice looking. She spoke with that bittersweet lilt of the Galicians which sounds charming to those of us from the South. For some reason I had been assigned to a more cheerful and larger room than Fernando's. After he complained bitterly about it, I offered to exchange rooms with him. He hesitated and finally walked out, throwing a leaden "No!" over his shoulder as he slammed the door. I unpacked a few things and went looking for him, hoping he'd want to take a stroll around the little town.

Bayona was not particularly picturesque. Most of its small stone houses were sturdy rather than attractive; they had been and would be there for a long time, that was certain. The Church of Santa Maria and the Collegiate Church were among the interesting public buildings we visited. Bayona's splendid view of the sea is what relieved the monotony of its town and justified its fame as a tourist spot.

Fernando Calleja, my irritable companion, took me to the home of a cousin—without specifying whether it was a close or a distant one. His name was Fernando also, Fernando Gallego, marquis of Quintanar and count of Santibañez del Rio, who had chosen Bayona as a summer retreat. A certain awkwardness in his walk was the result of an attack of polio suffered during childhood. We became good friends, Quintanar and I. He loved and understood all arts and had quite a flair for poetry. His verses were musical and sensitive; my guitar and I became the subjects of two of his poems—one of which was published in a collection many years ago.

Quintanar and I were often together that summer. At times I would bring my guitar over to his home and do my studying there. We had a tacit understanding: I would play one piece and he would read one of his poems, a new one, fresh from the oven, so to speak. His sweet, charming old mother just loved those exchanges between his poetry and my music. As for Calleja, he disappeared from Bayona, leaving a brief farewell note.

Quintanar and I met at La Barbeira beach each morning; he to swim a bit close to shore, I to dare swim out a lot farther. If the tall waves were breaking on the rock shoals of La Concheira, the next and more dangerous beach, we would delight in taking a small boat and row right into the surging billows beating on the sharp reefs, at the risk of overturning. When things would get too rough, we would return to our placid beach of La Barbeira and jump and duck into its calm waters, relishing our "escape."

One morning I had the scare of my life. Swimming out to sea, as usual, I suddenly caught a glimpse of an enormous fish not far from me. I swam away with all my strength, all the time wondering why the monster—a shark, I was sure—had not caught up with me yet. From the beach, Fernando Quintanar realized my predicament and immediately sent a motorboat to rescue me. As the sailor manning the craft approached me, he called out: "It's not a shark! It's a dolphin! Take it easy, don't run, he won't hurt you!" To me it was a voice from heaven. Being shortsighted and without glasses, I had not been able to tell one fish from the other. When the boat finally picked me up, I was doubly relieved: I was beginning to get a devastating cramp in my right leg from my attempt at championship swimming.

My young friend, Quintanar, a grandee of Spain, was often surrounded on the beach by the daughters of wealthy Galician families, all eager to win the grand prize in the local matrimony lottery. Marrying Fernando would have meant a considerable step up the social ladder. If at times he seemed to favor this girl or that, the others would swim away disdainfully and come to swim with me. My guitar and I were not considered a good "catch," but my stories and jokes made them laugh, a pleasant interlude in their quest for a title.

When I returned to Spain after World War II, I visited Fernando Quintanar in his apartment in Madrid, on the typical Plaza of Santa Barbara. The passing years had not been very kind to him, but he still had his liveliness and good humor and his clear, alert mind. I met his wife Elena, friendly, witty, attractive . . . all words that fail to fully describe that delightful woman.

As I write these lines of my autobiography—early in 1975

—I have just learned of the death of my dear, illustrious friend, Quintanar. His qualities enhanced his title, the reverse of the usual case. Another good and gentle friend—a gentleman to boot—has left this world. We have few enough of them to lose.

28

ONE AFTERNOON I WAS WALKING in Madrid with Helena
Hilinska, the unofficial niece of the Count and Countess of
Casa Miranda. I was escorting her down the narrow sidewalk
of Arenal Street on the way to the Plaza de Oriente. Helena
looked particularly beautiful that day. She always wore dark
clothes, made and fitted to enhance her slender, graceful figure.
This time she wore a short cape with a mink collar and a
diminutive hat trimmed with silk flowers. Quite a picture.

Helena walked ahead of me; the narrow sidewalk pre-
cluded our walking together. Passersby, coming the other way,
would separate us here and there. Suddenly a young ruffian,
apparently looking for both fun and trouble, threw his arms
around Helena and kissed her full on the mouth. All this happened in a twinkling of an eye. Helena pushed him away with
all her strength as soon as she recovered, just as I was rushing

towards her. Immediately, a circle of onlookers formed around us.

"I suppose you're the husband," sneered the man, looking me up and down. He was standing with his back to the plate-glass window of a store. I was on the outside of the sidewalk, near the curb. He came closer as if daring me, and then he touched my cheek. "What are you going to do about it?"

I was wearing a close-fitting cape, buttoned to my neck and open at the sides. I suppose the man thought I was easy to dispose of, like a wrapped-up package, with a simple push. From the right-side slit of my cape I let my arm fly toward him.

"Take this in the name of the young lady!" I punched him with such strength and accuracy that he fell backwards and went right through the plate-glass and landed on the floor of the display window. The owner came out, screaming. "You have to pay for this! Immediately!" He sent one of his clerks to look for a policeman.

The ruffian got up and came back to the sidewalk, nose bleeding profusely from the blow. He took out a switchblade knife and began opening it. And me, with only a fashionable thin walking stick in my hand! Two spectators jumped forward to stop him, just as two policemen arrived. They took the knife from him and began questioning us.

"I was a witness," volunteered a distinguished-looking man, stepping up to the policemen. "I saw it all," he said quietly. "Take this man to the station and let this young couple go."

The storekeeper intervened. "And who's going to pay for my broken window?"

The distinguished man kept telling him to wait, while he himself finished giving his account to the police officers. I stepped towards the storekeeper and told him I would take the responsibility of replacing his plate-glass. But after hearing the full testimony of the witness, he gave me a mild slap on the back, as if sending me on my way. "Not one more word, young fellow. I would have done the same. Go in peace."

One of the officers, impressed by the obvious self-assurance and authority of the witness, nevertheless attempted to follow regulations and asked the helpful man to identify himself. When they saw the card he showed them, both officers stood stiffly at attention and snapped: "Yes, sir!"

I stepped forward to thank him. He merely smiled and walked away—dropping his card in the storekeeper's hand as he passed him.

The officers wanted me to go with them to the station and sign a charge against my aggressor, but I asked them to take his knife away and let him go. They did not let him go; they took him with them, and if looks could kill, I would have been dead on the spot as he spat at me, "We'll meet again!"

All through the incident, Helena had stood on the same spot, remaining quiet and cool, as if she had not been a principal in the event but only an onlooker. I took her arm and headed towards Molinero's, the tea shop. There we sat silently, not a word crossed between us; all we did was drink our tea. I then took her home, to the residence of the Casa Mirandas. I walked her up one flight to the first-floor landing. Before going into the apartment, she threw her arms around my neck and gave me a kiss.

"That's all you need to say," I told her. "Good-bye."

Next day, Adelaida was on the phone earlier than usual. Her voice was so mellifluous and soft that I was immediately on my guard. Her usual telephone approach was carefree and full of fun. But, oh! that morning. . . .

"Bravo, Andrés! Congratulations! So, you almost got knifed defending the beautiful girl you were out with. I'm proud of you!"

"You certainly got the news fast. And probably distorted, too. Anyone else would have done the same in my place. I trust they also told you who the young lady was, and I'm sure you agree with me . . ."

"On the contrary," she interrupted. "Do you think I don't know what's going on between you two? Look, if you want to keep it up, in public or in private, go ahead. Luckily, my father leaves tomorrow to take up his new post in Cádiz, and mother and I will follow him in a few days."

The news hit me like a bombshell. In spite of my innocent wanderings as a young artist, Adelaida was the center of my world, the inspiration of my work and my plans for the future. Her photograph was in front of my eyes when I practiced and studied. I dreamed of no one else, awake or asleep.

It wasn't easy to convince her of all that, but at last she accepted my protestations of love, or pretended she did. In any case, we made up and the misunderstanding was forgotten. The squall was over and the sun shone again for us.

Señor Quesada sent for me to give me the good news I had been awaiting: it was time to set a date for my first tour of Argentina, Chile, and Uruguay. We agreed I would start the trip by the middle of next August.

I felt wonderful, knowing how important that jump across the ocean was for my career. I was going to play in sister nations whose cultural heritage was so closely allied to our own by history, religion, language . . . Still, those were new horizons for me, a new frontier to conquer for the guitar. I yearned to prove to friends and detractors alike that I was capable of enhancing the prestige of the art I had embraced outside of Spain, as well.

Needless to say, I was also dreaming of the day I could play in France, Germany, England, the principal targets of most young artists of those days. To me, especially, those countries meant a chance to meet and seek the approval and friendship of famous composers, concert artists, critics, impresarios. That —and luck—was an unbeatable combination of factors affecting a budding musical career. It all would come in time, I told myself. For now, I was happy beyond words at the prospect of visiting and playing in that fascinating cultural extension of Spain: South America.

Quesada sent the contract to me for my signature. When the messenger arrived, I was tempted to sign sight unseen and return it. Something held me back, perhaps some instinct inherited from my forefathers. Instead, I sent a note to Quesada, asking him to please come next day and fetch the signed document himself.

Of course, my first impulse was to tell Adelaida. Instead of reading the contract immediately, I put it away and ran to her pension. Carmen Rangel, the Mexican pianist, often let us meet briefly in her little apartment, reasonably safe from Madame Colonel's hostile presence. This time Carmen outdid herself in averting the lady's suspicions. She managed to get Adelaida to come with her to her place. The moment they walked in, I embraced Adelaida tenderly—while our hostess looked the other way.

"I've got the contract, darling! We'll be married as soon as I return from Buenos Aires! If your parents give you a hard time, move to your cousins'. From there you'll go directly to the church. You are over age; the law protects you. For the time being, save yourself their sermons, threats and pleas . . . I'll write to you as often as I can. Meanwhile, ask your cousins to help you get the necessary papers. One thing I insist on: I want to pay for your trousseau myself. At least, let's not have your parents spend a cent in our marriage."

Adelaida was overcome. I turned to Carmen; she understood. She smiled and went out on the balcony to watch the passing throngs.

It was our first kiss as sweethearts, nothing but the tender pressure of our burning lips. Others, more sensuous and mature ones as befit a man and a woman deeply in love, would come later.

"Andresillo, mother and I are leaving on the train for Cádiz tomorrow," she told me. "Father needs us to start a home for him at his new post. I'll try to get some kind woman to take care of your letters to me so mother won't know. Now leave, please. Mother'll be wondering what I'm doing here at Carmen's. She may suspect I'm with you and I want to save you both an unpleasant encounter. Please, go."

As soon as we broke our embrace, the door opened and in burst Madame Colonel. What fury! Her eyes were daggers when she saw me.

"Ah, just as I suspected! You are mad, Adelaida, stark mad! And you, Carmen, shame on you, lending yourself to this . . ."

"Come, mother, please," Adelaida told her, pulling her away to their own rooms.

I did not say a word, but I sent Adelaida a loving glance

and her mother an ironic smile in answer to her contemptuous look with which, no doubt, she meant to reduce me to dust.

When I returned to the pension, I found a message from Quesada. I called him back immediately and asked him to come and have lunch with me. As soon as he arrived, we went right into the dining room. Lunch hour was almost over and they were about to stop serving. I was beaming with optimism and he seemed to feel exactly the opposite. Obviously, there was something on his mind. As soon as we finished the brief meal, we went up to my room.

And then I sat down and began to read the contract, with Quesada watching me as I read clause after clause.

I finally burst out. "Señor Quesada, there isn't a clause in this contract that prevents your company from devouring my work and taking almost every cent I earn! What am I supposed to get from it all? The honor of being represented by the firm Quesada-Grassi? What am I going to live on? How much am I going to get paid? And, where will I get the money to reimburse you for the traveling expenses you so generously agree to advance? Apparently this contract means to tie me up for years and years without recourse. I'll just be accumulating a debt for traveling expenses! Even if my concerts were the financial success you've predicted, I'd wind up with nothing at the end!"

I thanked him for his interest in my career and reminded him I had never gone over the accounts after my concerts, eager to show confidence and appreciation, but . . .

"No, sir, after reading this contract I realize I've been a fool. No wonder you were sure I'd sign it! Here you are—take both copies and tear them up! Don't let anyone see them. A document like that can be as detrimental to the impresario as it would be to the artist who'd sign it."

I stood up and left, slamming the door behind me. In my distress, I had forgotten we were in my own room!

Walking the streets like an automaton, I saw all my dreams before me; the tour and success on which I had built the plans for my wedding, Adelaida's own expectations and the future I had anticipated for us both: foreign travels, comforts, interesting people . . . The whole thing had caved in on me like a sand castle. I was so deeply disappointed I did not have the heart to tell her the truth. Alleging a trip out of town, I did not see her before her departure for Cádiz with her family.

Four interminable weeks went by and not a word from Quesada. Several times I was tempted to pick up the phone and suggest that we go over the contract again and try to iron out its many difficulties with goodwill on both parts. But I was ashamed of giving in, and I stopped looking at the telephone.

One morning, along with my breakfast tray, the maid brought me a large, heavy envelope. My fingers shook as I tore it open. It contained a note from Quesada, a cable from his Buenos Aires associate, and . . . the contract.

The note read:

Señor Segovia:

My Buenos Aires associate, Señor Grassi, is a very difficult man to deal with. However, there is nothing I can do in South America without his cooperation. He has authorized me to modify most of the clauses in our agreement in terms more favorable to you. Read it now and don't delay letting me know if you find it acceptable. Your most cordial, etc. etc.

And now, the cable:

ANNOYED STOP WHATS SO GREAT ABOUT THAT GUITARIST STOP SUCCESS DOUBTFUL STOP OK OFFER HIM TRAVEL-ING EXPENSES PLUS THIRTY PERCENT BOXOFFICE IF NOT YOU TWO GET LOST

GRASSI

Difficult, indeed! At any rate, the new terms outlined in that delirious cablegram were the basis for a revised contract. The other clauses were negligible.

An employee of the pension took my answer to Quesada:

Here is the signed contract. I feel I am less of a slave now, with its new clauses. I have crossed out one which stipulates that I am to accept the exact terms for the next season. If in the first one I am as successful as you have predicted, I would rather sign a new agree-ment, even in Buenos Aires.

At that time the guitar was the Cinderella of all concert instruments. It seemed to me that the managerial firm I was bound to was a sort of main character in the tale: the wicked stepmother. All right, *another* principal in the story was preparing the rescue of the delicate damsel. Not Prince Charming, no. Only a young, enthusiastic artist who was capable of loving her, the guitar, of defending her and making her sing throughout his entire life:

Myself.

29

WHILE AWAITING CONFIRMATION from Buenos Aires, Quesada told me, he would set up some recitals for me in Catalonia, in the cities of Gerona, Reus, Manresa, Tarragona, and others. Knowing I would react favorably to the idea, he told me more about his plan.

"With part of the proceeds," he explained, "you and I could cover jointly the expenses of a concert at the great Palau of Music in Barcelona. Of course," he hastened to add, "your part of the investment would be considerably smaller."

I was not happy with the idea of suddenly becoming my own impresario, even in association with him. "I'll need all I can earn to buy clothes for the South American tour," I told him. "Why don't we stick to the same arrangement we've had till now? You give me what you consider reasonable. As for the Palau, I hope the manager hasn't forgotten how I filled his house with my concert some years back. He should be reminded that since then the guitar has achieved greater prominence in concert halls. If you throw that in next time you negotiate with him, you're bound to tip the balance and be able to reach a *fair* agreement for all three parts."

I emphasized the *fair*, hoping they wouldn't leave out the artist and just think of themselves.

During my first tours in Spain and abroad, I had to deal with all sorts of agents, most of them honest and considerate, but some of them unscrupulous operators who caught on quickly to my principal aim, in common with all budding artists: to be heard as often and by as many people as possible, to play for diversified audiences and have a broad exposure to the critics everywhere.

So great was my yearning to practice and display my art in public, that I was more than satisfied with whatever pittance I would earn at a concert—all the more if the audience had compensated me already with an ovation. My work was a labor of love, and success my greatest remuneration.

The unscrupulous impresario knew that only too well. In the case of a public concert, with box-office sale, he would manipulate the returns with such cunning that it seemed quite legitimate to pocket most of them himself, leaving the artist with little more than the satisfaction of his triumph onstage.

One victim of such a dishonest agent was a young cellist friend of mine, who would speak of his exploiter and end up by remarking wistfully, "I wonder what great surgeon cut out that man's conscience." It wasn't easy to remain in the concert field without meeting and even having to deal with that sort— one of which would deter any young artist from pursuing his career and his claim to fame.

We learned to live with that reality, so long as the agent helped us establish contact with musical organizations in Spain and abroad. In such arrangements there was little chance to cheat us, since the agent acted only as an intermediary, at a fixed commission of 10 percent of the fee in Europe and 20 percent overseas.

I, for one, have been lucky in that respect. I haven't found it too difficult to deal with agents. Three of them have been in charge of all my bookings: Conciertos Daniel in Spain and Spanish-America, from 1913 to 1956; Ibbs & Tillett, from 1924 to the present, for England and the Commonwealth; and Hurok Concerts for the vast territories of the United States and Canada, from 1943 to this day.

If on occasion I had problems with Conciertos Daniel, it was more due to misunderstandings with employees and associates than with Mr. Quesada himself. In every case, we always smoothed out our troubles in the end; between good will and a bad memory for the unpleasant, we each would do our part to restore harmony between us. On the other hand, in all my years of dealing with Ibbs & Tillet and Hurok Concerts I never had cause for concern; not once have *I* had to question their handling of my concerts and details, financial or otherwise.

It would not be fair to leave the subject without noting that many prominent musicians at the peak of their fame have made life miserable for their agents and managers. Two such cases come to mind.

One day in London, I was waiting for Mr. Tillett to arrive at my hotel. I was surprised he was so late; he was always so punctual and considerate. When he at last arrived, I noticed he was upset. I could see it in the tense expression on his face.

"What's wrong?" I asked him, as he dropped wearily on an arm chair.

"Rachmaninoff," he answered. "He called me a couple of hours ago. I went flying to see him, and the moment I got to his room I knew something was wrong. He was pacing up and down like a caged lion, brandishing a copy of the *London Times*. His eyes had a wild look; his voice was strained with anger. 'Look at this ad!' he exclaimed. 'It was placed by your office. Read it!'

"I read it," continued Mr. Tillett, "but I couldn't see anything wrong with it.

"I raised my head to him with a questioning look. 'Can't you see?' Rachmaninoff shouted. 'They've got my name in the same size print as that of the conductor. I am the soloist! That shows the little respect you and your associates have for me!'

"Well, I bowed and left, and here I am, Maestro Segovia," concluded Mr. Tillett, still visibly upset.

175

"You English are too restrained," I told him, trying to calm him down. "A Latin would have shouted Rachmaninoff down, and the whole thing would have ended in a Spanish free-for-all."

"How does that end, Mr. Segovia?" he asked, quite serious and interested.

"I don't know!" I burst out laughing.

Another case of an artist-tyrant vis-à-vis his manager was that of a famous cellist and my first manager in the United States, Coppicus—no one ever called him by any other name, I can't even remember what it was. Poor Mr. Coppicus could count on one infallible disaster each season: reviewing accounts with the eminent cellist. Oh, they were the best of friends all year round, to be sure. Everything was fine between them until time came to look at those accounts. For no reason whatsoever! Year in and year out, nothing was wrong with them. However, every time, the cellist would arrive at Coppicus' office already looking like a prosecuting attorney. For the rest of the afternoon they would remain locked in, going over the most picayune details, none of them worth the time and trouble of those two important men—each famous the world over in his field. At the end of the season, both exhausted, would shake hands and resume their cordial relationship for the rest of the year.

Yes, some artists—particularly renowned ones—can drive managers and impresarios to distraction with whims and fits of temper and even frequent defaults on the terms of contracts signed in good faith. Managers and impresarios are not the only ones who take advantage of the prestige and their power. Goodwill works—or should work—both ways.

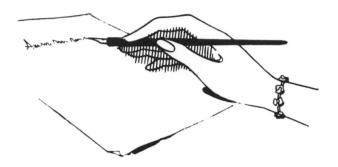

30

My series of recitals in Catalonia was over, and I returned to Madrid one morning. There was a message for me at the pension—from Adelaida's cousins! I didn't even go up to my room—I dropped my baggage in the lobby and ran to the phone. One of Adelaida's relatives—Teresa, pretty and kind, I had been told—answered.

"I have a letter for you from Adelaida. I got it two days ago," she informed me.

"If you forgive me," I said, "I won't even ask you to receive me. Give it to your maid or to the doorman to hand it to me. I'll pass by to pick it up in a few minutes."

I asked the porter at the pension to take my things to my room—and mind he didn't drop my guitar. I ran to the nearest hackstand to hail a carriage—motorcabs were still rare in those days. A fat little man prevented me from boarding an available coach. He jumped on the running board himself and shouted at the coachman, "Hey, chum, drop your awning and get on like lightning to the Retiro Park."

The coachman, half-asleep and ill-humored as all coachmen were, answered angrily, "Who do you think you are, speaking to me in the familiar *tú*. Maybe you've eaten from the same bucket of oats with my horse, but from the same plate with me . . . never! And what's that 'chum' business about? I never saw you before in my life, I'm not your chum, and I ain't going to drop my awning and go nowhere with you. Scat!"

At that unexpected harangue, the little man jumped down from the running board and said, half-embarrassed: "Sorry, kid, I am from Cuba. There we speak in *tú* to everyone except the bishop!"

"Well, here in Madrid we're more dignified!" spat the coachman.

With all the dignity I could muster in my anxiety to get that letter, I approached the coachman. "I beg you, sir, to have the kindness to take me to the Street of Alcalá number 84, if you will." I then turned to the Cuban and pointed an approaching free cab about to pull into the hackstand. "There's your chance—better luck this time."

Once we were trotting along leisurely, I tapped the coachman's seat. "Dear friend," I told the irritable driver, "couldn't you hurry a bit? Tell your horse I have a letter from my sweetheart waiting for me, maybe he'll understand."

It didn't do much good, but we got there eventually. I paid and jumped down to the sidewalk. And then I thought: "What will these people say if they see me for the first time as I am now, unkempt, unshaven, in rumpled clothes after the trip, smelling of train fumes? How terrible, for me and—for Adelaida!"

I was about to retrace my steps, but the anxiety to read her letter won. I walked up the stairs.

Surely, they must have been watching from the balcony, and when they saw me get out of the coach they supposed that it was I. The moment I rang the bell, the maid came out, the letter in her hand and a mischievous look on her face.

First Letter from Adelaida, 1919

Andresillo:

Mother and I are dead tired after moving to Cádiz and setting up a home again. How I miss my rocking chair and my straw fan! (Remember mother and I are from the Pearl of the Antilles, Cuba.) This old house must have been occupied by recluses, or maybe not occupied at all. The junk we had to throw out! We hired a couple of strong women to help us and our regular maid, but . . . these Andalusians! Both of them spent the time telling stories and making us laugh. What picturesque people. One of them wears a small bunch of flowers right on top of her head, as if the thing had grown up there! And she's no chicken, but she certainly enlivens her years with her cheerful looks and disposition. Must go now, will continue this later.

Darling, I left this off two days ago, but today I am going to finish this letter. I've locked myself up in my room so I can have this "chat" with you. Now, read on and don't go to sleep . . . unless you're going to dream about me.

And now I want to tell you about Alejo and his wife, the couple who have been assigned to us as orderlies. They are about fifty, they work for the military in this zone. He is a petty officer in the infantry, now retired. Both of them seem to like me . . . and to detest my father! Poor Papa scares everyone with that voice and those manners. No one can stand him and . . . he knows it. He is always fuming when he gets home. Mother tries to pacify him, but it's no use. The moment he sets his eyes on me, he remembers you and his blood boils. Then, suddenly, he jumps from rage to tenderness and tries to embrace me, always sighing but unable to say a word. I feel sorry for him. He really thinks I am going to be the world's unhappiest woman with you. He moves me so at times I wish I could please him and break our engagement. (Now, don't you flare up.)

I am happy to tell you that I have spoken to Manuela— Alejo's wife, the orderly—about you, and she offers to take care of your letters to me and see that I get them without my family learning about them. Just write me to Alejo's name and don't you dare put yours on the return address. You would get us all in trouble; Alejo, Manuela, and me. At least we've solved that problem, darling.

Ships to Buenos Aires and Montevideo leave from Cádiz, I suppose you know. Do I have to tell you what is on my mind? When you come to Cádiz to board yours, make sure your name is not mentioned in the local newspapers.

We were visited yesterday by an uncle of mine, my mother's brother. From my first conversation with him it was obvious that

Andrés Segovia. Lithograph by Helmut Ruhermann, Madrid 1919.

mother had asked him to try to find out how I feel about you, whether we are still engaged, what are your plans and, above all, if you are coming to Cádiz. Needless to say, I didn't open my mouth—other than to steer him wrong.

Alejo's wife just told me that my uncle has issued orders to the staff to give him any letter that arrives for me. Don't worry, Alejo himself is in charge of picking up the mail at the post office. Still, I shan't rest until we have established regular contact.

Tell me all about your tour in Catalonia; your programs, what the critics said, the pretty girls you met, etc. Good-bye, Andresillo, and receive all my love. Forever yours,

Adelaida

My darling Adelaida:

It made me so happy to receive your letter, although it would have been infinitely more welcome had you written about what is in your heart, the excitement of our engagement, and other intimate feelings and details—rather than external matters.

Reading your letter I decided to make sure I keep it always, so I can compare it with the ones you'll write to me, say, thirty years from now. By then—at the epilogue of our love, when tenderness would have replaced ardor—such temperate tone will be called for. But . . . how should I interpret this one I have received now?

Perhaps your restraint is due to fear that this letter would fall into your parents' hands, in which case I understand, of course. I, too, will abstain from expressing freely my feelings for you. How these pages would overflow with love words if I could repeat the things I say to you in my mind! Well, then, to other matters.

You say that the couple who work for your family in Cádiz have offered to help us communicate with one another. Are you sure that may not be your mother's ruse to intercept our letters? Wouldn't this Alejo and his wife be feigning loyalty to you against your father just to gain your trust and confidence? I wonder if he, a petty officer under military jurisdiction, would risk disobeying and contradicting a high superior to that extent. Do be careful.

My concerts in Catalonia were only mildly successful. I played in Sabadell, Tarrasa, and other small towns. The one positive aspect was my fee, which nurtured my very lean wallet just in time. I did not give a concert in Barcelona, after all. The Palau Theater was booked solid until the middle of next month and I could not wait that long for an open date.

But I got to see Dr. Quiroga and his family in Barcelona. The seraphic Doña Filomena of whom I've told you so much, is very ill and getting weaker. The worst is expected by now. Heaven should get ready to receive an angel who has been more than seventy years on this earth.

I saw a young guitarist, a pupil of Fortea, whom I had met some years back through Carlos Verger, the professor of engraving at the Royal Academy of Fine Arts. The young musician launched his career at Barcelona's Mozart Hall. In my opinion he was not ready to play in public, but he was anxious to give his first recital, and so he had come to see me. I was retranscribing *Leyenda* by Albéniz, which hereto has been played from the transcription made by that hack, Don Severino García. Well, the young guitarist asked me to teach it to him, he wanted to make it the *pièce de résistance* in his projected recital. Every morning around eight he would come to my pension to review his program and in particular *Leyenda*. Once he mentioned the poor sale of tickets that so far was reported at the Mozart's box office. I asked him to bring me a couple of dozens to sell among my friends. Needless to say, I didn't collect for them. They were cheap enough, so my expense was negligible

The day of the concert the young fellow was nervous, insecure. He played the difficult passages very poorly. When the program was over, I went back to see him. He was very disappointed. "How fortunate you are, Andrés!" he told me. "Why?" I asked. "Look at the poor attendance I had," he explained. "When you play, you fill the hall." I couldn't help think that luck is the name mediocre artists give to success. You notice, dear Adelaida, that I have not mentioned his name.

Of course I know that the ship that will take me to South America stops in Cádiz, and I already have a plan for us to meet. It's been some years since I played in Cádiz, so I doubt many will recognize me. I'll take the train four or five days before I have to board my ship, and I will register at a pension under another name. Let me know if there is a guard posted near your house. Maybe we can talk through some grille at a surrounding little street—I suppose that big house occupies the entire block. I am afraid only that some passerby will see us and tell your parents.

Make sure you test the loyalty of Alejo and his wife. The best thing would be for the wife to open some back door and let me in so we can talk while she watches. Explore that possibility with all your cunning and let me know. You have plenty of time—it'll be a couple of months before I have to take that ship from Cádiz.

I am so hungry for you I can hardly concentrate on anything except on thoughts of you. Even when I work, my fingers falter if you come to my mind. When I am with friends, I fall suddenly silent, remembering your eyes, your voice. They ask me if I've fallen asleep with my eyes open. In short, darling, you are the center of my universe.

However, when I want to cool off, I pick up your letter and read it again. A friend told me this story the other day: A young man, madly in love, told his sweetheart: "I love everything about you, I love even your shadow. And you, darling, what do you like most about me?" And the girl replied: "Your good taste." Are you like that girl, Adelaida?

That is all for now. I am anxious to know if this letter reached you. It is my first one. Number yours, too.

Andrés

31

BACK IN MADRID I had the pleasure of getting together with my cellist friend, Gaspar Cassadó. He was returning from concerts in Oviedo and Gijón and, was stopping in Madrid for a couple of days before going back home to Barcelona.

We had talked in the past about going together some day to Granada. Gaspar had never been in the beautiful Andalusian city.

"Have you a concert coming up soon?" I asked him.

"No," he answered.

"Can you spend three weeks in Granada, then?"

"Granada? I'd cancel a half dozen concerts for the chance!"

"Bravo! Let's go to the central telephone office and let my friends know we're coming."

I called Miguel Cerón, my childhood friend—the one who had negotiated my first guitar for me, that old Ferrer I used to practice on behind my uncle's back. I told Miguel of my plan: Gaspar and I would give three concerts in Granada for the Art Center.

". . . And let the president of the club know we won't be asking for a fee. All we want is to cover the fare and the pension bill. That pittance will be easy enough to make with three concerts at the little theater, the Alhambra Palace. What do you think, Miguel?"

"Yes, yes! Fine! Come! It won't be difficult to arrange."

"All right." I went on to give him advice I knew he didn't need. "Don't let the members of our group over there start procrastinating. Ask them to help you. First of all, try to get the little theater for nothing, with lights and ushers thrown in. And make sure we get good publicity. Go, now. We'll be waiting to hear from you."

However, in our youthful optimism we had forgotten one important detail. Suddenly Gaspar remembered and slapped his forehead.

"Hey! Who's going to accompany my cello? No professional pianist will play for a mythical fee, especially if he's already booked to play somewhere for those nights."

"My God, you're right!"

We were silent and worried only a few minutes. The same name came to our lips at the same time:

"Gabriel Abreu!"

Abreu was a young Madrid architect who had a passion for music and had studied piano seriously. No professional pianist could do better in the emergency. Also, his financial situation was not pressing, to say the least. We were sure he would join us in that small adventure. We called him up.

Of course he would play with us, he said immediately. Moreover, in the unlikely event that the recitals wouldn't cover our expenses, he himself would take care of them.

"Thank you, Gabriel," I told him. "My friends over there will get Granada's public to attend the recitals, they are hungry enough for music. Gaspar's name is becoming known in the provinces and you, with your talent and personality, will contribute to this joint effort. We can't help but succeed."

Cerón's reports, too, were most encouraging. Even before

the programs were announced, tickets were flying, just on the strength of our reputation.

Early one morning we took the Madrid-Seville express, with connections at the town of Baeza for Granada. The trip entailed traveling on two different railroad companies, and it so happened that both were involved in a dispute for certain rights and privileges. Andalusians being Andalusians, the southern company decided to pressure their competitors into negotiating for a settlement. How? By making things as uncomfortable as possible for passengers coming in on the northern carrier. They would start rolling the train for Granada just as the one from the north was arriving at Baeza, the changing point. No matter how they ran, rushed, and shouted desperately, passengers in transit were unable to board that train for the south. There it was, in front of their eyes, pulling away amidst a clatter of bells and whistles, celebrating the cruel joke with great jets of black smoke. Too bad—the train from the north was late, as ever. Andalusian trains arrive and depart on time, was the lesson they were driving home.

We had no alternative but to pile up our instruments and bags into a decrepit horse-drawn coach and head for Baeza to spend the night. We telephoned the Arts Center and notified them we would be taking the morning train to Granada. They were disappointed we would not be arriving that same day.

We did not waste that unscheduled stop at historic Baeza —or Biesa, as it was called centuries ago by the Saracens. We had an excellent guide in our architect-pianist, Gabriel Abreu. He took us to see the old streets, plazas, monuments, and ruins, vestiges of the grandeur of the once-powerful citadel surnamed The Hawk's Nest because of its lofty height, perched above the Guadalquivir, with a breathtaking view of the verdant plains at its feet.

When we got to the station the next morning, the cardboard clock at our platform already marked the scheduled departure of our train for Granada. Preparations for departure at provincial stations were comical in Spain at that time. First the stationmaster would shake the tongue of a bell in accelerated monochords. Then came three distinct ominous peals. Nothing happened. In a little while, a railroad employee would

186

Portrait of Segovia by Muñoz Lucena, Granada 1918.

run the length of the platform like a madman, ringing a strident handbell all the way. Another wait. The same man, on his way back, would run, shouting wildly: "Passengers, board your train!" Another wait; be patient. Now the same man went back, retracing his steps, this time furiously slamming shut the wagon doors. Nothing happened. At last, the stationmaster would take a strategic position in the center of the platform, produce a formidable metal whistle, and blow long, penetrating trills with all his might. A few more minutes of breathless expectation. Finally, flanked by steam jets on each side, the engine would wail painfully as it began to move, creaking at all articulation points until the wheels gained momentum and drowned out all surrounding noise. It was because of all that tomfoolery at departure that trains were guaranteed to be at least fifteen minutes late arriving from provincial depots.

We got to Granada dog-tired and starving. Miguel Cerón and a few members of the Arts Center took us immediately to the Hotel Paris. Once refreshed, we left our modest rooms and took to the streets. Gaspar was avidly taking in the sights, ahing and ohing, left and right as he passed famous landmarks. Gabriel and I bridled our enthusiasm, saving it all for the Alhambra.

"I think you'll have a full house at all three concerts," Miguel told us gleefully. "The first one is already sold out. Seats for the second and third are going fast. Concertgoers love the program."

To give each one an equal chance for personal success, we decided to begin the first concert with Gabriel Abreu, then a short pause, and then I would play. A long interval, and Gaspar Cassadó would close, accompanied, of course, by Abreu. The procedure would be reversed accordingly in the other two concerts.

The first concert in Granada was a success in every way for all three of us. Artistically as well as financially. Perhaps the public felt more sympathy for our youthful efforts than admiration for our still-developing merits as performing artists. Whatever it was, the night was successful.

At first, Gabriel Abreu was very nervous on stage. He had seldom played in public. He started by muddling his chords and arpeggios, by rushing his tempos and skipping notes in his scales. Gaspar and I, listening offstage, got panicky. We were afraid the public would feel cheated and end up by rejecting us altogether. Moreover, we feared that our anguish and concern would influence our own playing, when time came for our turn. However, Gabriel calmed down and regained his confidence in the Beethoven sonata. He played it with a much easier technique and gave it a definite style in his interpretation. We breathed, at last, when we heard the long applause he received at the end, and our fears vanished instantly. In fact, Gabriel had to add two Scarlatti sonatas and a Chopin mazurka for encores.

I was sandwiched between the ample fortes of the piano and what followed me: the mellow voice of the cello, warm and vigorous, as Tita Ruffo would have wished for himself. I managed to fare well, nevertheless. I even thought I heard a soft "hum" of approval from Mozart, Schumann, Sor, Albéniz and Granados, whose compositions made up my part of the program. Perhaps more due to the poetry which the guitar imparts to those works than to my interpretation.

The hero of the night was Gaspar with his cello. Although there was always a perfect unity between him and his beautiful instrument, his smiling, friendly appearance first won the public's sympathy and, immediately after, its respect. He would turn serious and mature-looking the moment he tackled the first notes. There was dignity and concentration in his manner; in the emotional or intricate passages, he would close his eyes instinctively and follow the emotion of the music with a slight frown. The public just couldn't help listening with respect and admiration. There was that perfect sound coming from his cello, something the Granadinos were not fortunate enough to hear very often. He surprised and ignited the audience. That night he received long waves of fervent, solid applause.

Gaspar and I had rehearsed two transcriptions for guitar and cello, *Granada* and *Torre Bermeja*, both by Albéniz. At the end of the scheduled program we went out together on stage. It was then that Gaspar began his ill-advised habit of speaking in public. He stepped up front and gave them a little speech woven with a mixture of Catalan and Andalusian expressions,

thanking the audience for their generous reception and inform-
ing them of the extra works we had prepared for them.

His words found some sympathetic reception in the public.
As for me, I was biting my lip, amused and annoyed at the
same time.

The following two recitals were as well attended as the
first one, and as well received. Some of our friends even proposed that we give a fourth one, but I was against it. "Let's not
overstay our welcome," I said, seconded by Gabriel and Gaspar.

Non-Andalusian Gabriel and Gaspar were taken by my
friends to see the city's many interesting and picturesque sights,
to visit its dreamy villas and meet its distinguished tenants.
They were surrounded by attractive and admiring young people
and beautiful girls wherever they went. It was wonderful to see
them both, impressed and delighted beyond words, when they
saw the Alhambra, the Generalife, the most picturesque nooks
and corners of the Albaicín and other "musts" for artists and
poets who visit Granada.

We were not going to risk being told indirectly, as Granada did to poet Zorrilla last century, "Bard, depart!" when *he*
overstayed his welcome. We took a day train and returned to
Madrid. There were two foreign tourists in the compartment
with us, returning from their first visit to Granada. The one
who spoke better Spanish expressed their enthusiasm with
these few words: "I, myself, am from Amsterdam, a beautiful
city, but I assure you that, after seeing Granada, I wish I had
been born here." To that, a native who overheard the conversation burst in with the thickest Andalusian accent: "Me,
gentlemen, why . . . I would have died of shame if I hadn't
been born in Granada!" All of us burst out laughing. Soon the
chauvinistic Granadino parted from us in Baeza, the next station. Donning his hat at a rakish angle, he turned to us from
the compartment door and bade us farewell with an Olympian
gesture: "Go with God and have a good journey!" all the time
rolling his eyes in commiseration, for he wouldn't have continued that journey outside his province of Granada for
Madrid or, indeed, the whole world!

There were two letters awaiting me at the pension Marlasca—by then practically my permanent residence in Madrid. One was an urgent summons from Quesada, my manager, and the other a letter from Adelaida, forwarded to me by her cousin, Teresa Canga-Argüelles. I don't have to tell the reader which one I opened first.

Her letter started angry, even aggressive, and ended up tenderly. She informed me that the windows of her house within the military complex in Cádiz were so high that we'd have to shout to each other if I went to speak with her behind her parents' back, as was my plan. Seeing each other eye to eye was out of the question: the window was that high above the street. I got the bright idea of buying a pair of picador stirrups, the kind that accommodate the whole foot—a solid support, I thought. I would tie the stirrups to a sturdy rope and pass the rope through one of the window bars, so I could step into the things and thus shorten the distance separating me from Adelaida's window . . . and her lips.

Her answer to that suggestion was a categorical "No!" To open her window at night and speak to a man would be folly; next morning all of Cádiz as well as her family and her friends would hear about it and she would be disgraced—to say nothing of what would happen to Alejo's wife for having aided the tryst as a "lookout." "It is best that I come out on the front balcony of my house in the morning or the afternoon—we will arrange the hour—and you pass by on the street. We will look at one another and let our eyes speak our thoughts," was her suggestion. We didn't write again about *that*, but . . . I had my own ideas.

In his letter, Quesada informed me that his Buenos Aires representative, Mr. Grassi, wanted to advance the dates of my concerts. No use waiting until the concert audiences had spent all their money in the many events that were being advertised already; great concert stars would precede me if I didn't advance my dates.

"Then when do I sail?" I asked Quesada when we met.

"Middle of June," he said. "And Grassi is asking for eight different programs."

"Eight different programs!" I repeated, alarmed, all the time thinking, Where was I going to get over one hundred compositions? The guitar repertoire hardly yielded enough material for two recitals.

"I have your round-trip ticket," Quesada went on, "deluxe class, on the S/S *Queen Victoria*."

"That "deluxe" was a publicity stunt of the steamship company. If that was deluxe, one wondered what third class would be like.

"I would like to sail from Cádiz," I said. What difference would it make? The ship stopped there before crossing the Atlantic.

He made a face and, good impresario that he was, he became intrigued, wondering if I was booking myself to play in Cádiz, as I had done, without his participation, on the three Granada concerts. "Are you planning a performance in Cádiz on your own?" he asked.

"On the contrary. I don't want it known that I'll be there, so my fiancée and I can say good-bye without interference from her parents. They don't approve."

"That spoils the publicity we wanted to give your departure so the news would reach Buenos Aires and start helping us there."

"Believe me, Señor Quesada," I argued, "the success of my tour doesn't depend on the modest notices the press in Madrid or Barcelona may publish about my departure, but on the reception my guitar and I receive in those countries from knowledgeable concertogoers."

He smiled and finally agreed with me. Before we parted, he advised me, "Start getting all the papers you'll need to get your visa at the Argentine consulate. It's all very complicated; use whatever contacts you can think of in that direction."

I thought of one, Roberto Levilier, the Argentine diplomat who a few years back had offered me his help if I ever thought of visiting his country. I found out he now was the *chargé d'affaires* at his embassy.

I wrote him a note, reminding him of our day at Bacarisas' studio, etc. In a few lines I explained why I wanted to see him. His answer came back immediately, giving me an appointment to see him in a couple of days. We met and he wrote on my passport: "A very esteemed friend of this embassy," and signed it and affixed the official seal. That alone saved me trips to Málaga, Jaén, Linares, Córdoba, etc., to look for such certificates as these: attesting that neither my parents nor my grandparents had ever had a venereal disease, mental disorder, or a jail sentence; attesting that the entire family had certificates of good conduct from the police of every city we ever lived in; all that plus the guarantee of a Buenos Aires bank regarding the solvency of the firm that was booking me there, and proof of a return ticket to Spain. I was so grateful to my friend Lavilier for saving me that awful mess, I thanked him in a letter written on board ship.

Lavilier didn't stop there. To his special visa, he added the several letters of introduction to some of Buenos Aires' most important people, and one personal one to me which he ended with these words: "I am sure my friends will give you a warm welcome and share with me the pleasure of hearing you transform the guitar into a noble concert instrument." He closed with this revealing sentence which clearly told me the reason for his deferential treatment: "I was talking about you the other day with the Duke of Bivona, at a cocktail party. You have a fine friend in him."

Lavilier's letters did help me, indeed, in Buenos Aires.

32

Federico Moreno Torroba

IN THE DAYS PRECEDING my departure from Spain, correspondence with Adelaida became quite regular, thanks to the loyalty of Alejo and his wife, who took care of receiving my letters and posting hers to me. Hers became more loving, and mine increasingly passionate.

Then there was a "first" in the field of the guitar: For the first time, a composer who was not a guitarist wrote a piece for the guitar. It was Federico Moreno Torroba, whose musical poem had just been premiered by the National Symphony under the direction of Maestro Arbós. Moreno Torroba had been introduced to me by the orchestra's first violin, Señor Francés. It did not take us long to become friends, nor for him to accede to my suggestion: Would he compose something for the guitar? In a few weeks he came up with a slight but truly beautiful *Dance in E Major*. In spite of his scant knowledge of the guitar's complex technique, he approached it accurately by sheer instinct, and to my joy the work remained in the repertoire. That success prompted Manuel de Falla to compose his very beautiful *Homage*, and Joaquín Turina his splendid *Sevillana*. Then Torroba again took up his pen in behalf of the guitar and composed a graceful sonatina, also dedicated to me and another jewel of our repertoire. The abovementioned *Dance in E Major* in time became part of Torroba's *Suite Castellana*, joining the other components of the suite, the *Fandanguillo* and the *Arada*. These last two Torroba composed after my return from South America. But . . . back to my last days in Spain then.

Four days before the S/S *Queen Victoria* was scheduled to sail from Cádiz, I took a train for that Andalusian city. On arrival, I engaged a room at a modest and quiet pension, under the name of Antonio Fernández. From Madrid, I had advised Adelaida of my scheduled arrival and even set a date for our first meeting—at 1:00 A.M.!

There I was, on the way to her house, asking passersby for directions. If I remember correctly, her house was the only building on the block. I walked around it, looking up to see which window had been left open. Adelaida's little hand came out from one of them and dropped a small envelope. Quickly, I picked it up and walked over to the corner to read it under the street lamp:

Andrés:

I am very nervous. We won't be able to speak. If mother discovers that I am not in my room, she is bound to be alarmed and wake up father. I shudder to think what would happen. Please go. Throw me a note with your address, and I will send Alejo to your pension tomorrow. Adios. Love.

I ran back under the window and hissed softly, calling her. After long minutes, she replied. I had already taken my stirrups out of the package and now I hurled the rope tied to one of them up against the wrought-iron grille.

"Tie this rope to the window with two knots!" I whispered as loud as I could. She tied it. "Now, tie this other one," I told her, as I cast the other rope toward her. She did. I stepped into the lowest stirrup, the one closest to me, and grasping the

195

Drawing by Miguel del Pino y Sardá
for a recital by Andrés Segovia
in Madrid, 1920.

wrought-iron grille I climbed into the second one, one step higher. "Thank God, I can see you now! But, wait! I've come prepared with everything," I told her. Out of my pocket, I took a small flashlight, focusing the beam on her beautiful face.

For a long time I looked at her, until our lips met. I could have remained perched on that window for an eternity, but, alas, a couple of drunks happened to pass by just then.

"Ha! A prowler. Let's cut the ropes and bring him down!"

"We haven't got a knife."

"Then, let's tell the night watchman."

"Yes! The fool's trying to get into that house by squeezing through the window grille. Ha, ha, ha . . ."

They were too drunk to carry out their threats, but the incident had thrown Adelaida into a panic. "Andrés, please, please! Get back down, quickly!"

I did, more to calm her down than out of fear of being discovered.

"I can't untie the knots!" she whispered now, crying desperately. Of course she couldn't; my weight had tightened the knots fast.

"Call Alejo!" I almost screamed.

"My God, what a disgrace! And at this hour!" she whimpered as she disappeared from view.

I stopped at the corner and looked back to see if they had succeeded in untying the ropes. In a few minutes I heard the clinking of the stirrups against the wrought-iron grille. They were hoisting them up, at last.

I headed back to my pension. Well, not exactly. I had forgotten both the way and the name of the street I had to reach, so for almost three hours I wound my way through Cádiz's little plazas and twisting and turning old streets. The first sixty minutes I felt as if I were returning from another planet, my feet rambling *ad caprice,* my mind and heart fixed still on the memory of my beloved's face, on her looks and kisses.

It was dawn when I finally recognized one of the streets I had walked on the way to the brief meeting and at last I reached the pension. I rang the doorbell seven or eight times, but no one opened. I decided to continue walking toward the port and wait until one of the waterfront taverns opened. At the first one that gave a sign of life, I asked for toast and a glass of local brandy. There I sat, with my thoughts, until a nearby clock rang eight and I went back to my modest lodgings.

Stretched out in bed I tried to dream rather than sleep, but after the emotions and the long walks, exhaustion soon set in and I closed my eyes. I woke up quite late and looked for the maid. After convincing her with a generous tip, I sent her to fetch Alejo with the brief message that "his friend from Madrid was waiting." He'd understand who the "friend" was.

In a couple of hours he showed up at the pension, a reserved man of few spontaneous words. His reticence and terse answers gave me the impression he was now making others pay for years of submission to despotic chiefs during his military life. I could see it in his mechanical gesture of respect when some mention was made of captain this and colonel that, in his sudden change to an authoritarian tone the few times he referred to sergeants and corporals or poor recruits.

For a long time I discussed with him the possibility of saying farewell to Adelaida without risking the perils we had suffered the previous night. We agreed that there was no other way but to follow my original plan: to go into the house after midnight and spend a few minutes talking with my fiancée under the kind sponsorship of his good wife. After suggesting some exaggerated precautions, he finally agreed.

I was afraid anything at this point could spoil the plan, and so I asked him not to open the small envelope I gave him until he got home. There were three hundred *pesetas* inside, with a note asking him to buy a nice present for his wife in Adelaida's name and mine.

I cannot describe the emotions of that farewell; the sorrow of having to leave my beloved behind, the uncertainty of what could await me across that ocean that was to separate me from my country, the thought of my mother's precarious future if my tour were to fail, the idea of arriving in a new land, after seventeen days at sea, without loved ones to meet . . .

The moment I boarded ship I dropped my things in my cabin and went up on deck, a knot in my throat, to watch our departure. People were screaming to one another, from deck to pier, the usual things . . . "Adios . . . Bon voyage . . . My love to so-and-so . . . Don't forget to write . . . Come back soon . . . ! " I walked away from them to a quiet spot. There I watched the coast of Cádiz, wrapped in fog, until it became just a length of gray ribbon in the horizon.

I couldn't hold back my tears any longer. I cried quietly, trying to still a frenzied voice in my heart that said, "Go back!" Suddenly I doubted the outcome of that trip, its very purpose, the honesty of my agents, the quiet, beautiful sea and sky, the ship, everything!

A voice behind me brought me back. "It's hard to leave home, isn't it?" someone said to me softly and kindly. I turned around fast and saw an aging gentleman, friendly and dignified at the same time. "Calm yourself, young man, and get your spirits back. You are going to need them to win the fight ahead of you out there in the world. I know who you are, although I haven't heard you play. You have friends and admirers awaiting you in Buenos Aires, and forgive me if I seem to intrude in your thoughts."

I broke the silence that followed. "Thank you, sir, for comforting me. It's the first time I've left Spain. I am not a pessimist, but I leave behind loved ones and others who depend on me. I was thinking of them. . . ."

The old gentleman fixed his kind look on me. "Allow me to introduce myself," he said after a moment. "My name is Juan Martínez Roig. I live in Tucumán, Northern Argentina. I am what you could call a retired successful businessman. Allow me to be your first friend in the New World."

ANDRÉS SEGOVIA
28–IV–1976
Madrid

Index

Index